Decoys of Maritime Canada

by Dale and Gary Guyette

Schiffer Publishing Ltd

Box E, Exton, Pennsylvania 19341

Books on decoys and other related subjects available from Schiffer Publishing Ltd., are:

American Bird Decoys
American Factory Decoys
The Art of the Decoy
Blue Ribbon Pattern Series
Decoys of the Mid-Atlantic Region
Decoys of the Mississippi Flyway
Factory Decoys
New England Decoys
New Jersey Decoys
Shore Bird Decoys
Prairie Wings
Waterfowl Carving, Blue Ribbon Techniques

Library of Congress Catalog Number 82–62953

Printed in the United States of America.
ISBN: 0-916838-76-5
Published by Schiffer Publishing Ltd.

Designed by Ellen J. Taylor

Schiffer Publishing Ltd.
Box E
Exton, Pennsylvania 193419990

To our daughter Kendall, who since her birth, has logged nearly as many miles as her parents have in researching the information for this book.

QUEBEC
TABUSINTAC
NEW BRUNSWICK
PRINCE EDWARD ISLAND
SAINT JOHN
MAINE
BAY OF FUNDY
NOVA SCOTIA
HALIFAX
BOSTON
CAPE COD
N
ATLANTIC OCEAN

Table of Contents

Acknowledgments

Many people helped us put this book together. We especially want to thank John McKay, Deputy Minister of Tourism for the province of New Brunswick. John contributed much valuable information from his own independant research on New Brunswick decoys and their carvers. The New Brunswick Chapter includes numerous excerpts from his notes. We also wish to thank the following people for their cooperation and assistance:

Mr. and Mrs. Gerald Anderson, George Ashton, Mr. and Mrs. Foster Baker, Mr. and Mrs. Jim Baker, Steven Baker, Bob Bancroft, Clay and Carol Benson, Mr. and Mrs. Douglas Bezanson, Paul Breau, Sammy Breau, Mr. and Mrs. Stacy Bryanton, Cyril Bulgar, Mr. and Mrs. Angus Byers, Ron Cameron, Mr. and Mrs. Ron Casselman, George and Muriel Champion, Mr. and Mrs. Arthur Clark, Mr. and Mrs. Chris Cooper, Paul and Diana Crosland, Oscar and Beryl Crowell, John and Shirley Delph, Gerard Doucett, Mrs. Ivan Duggan, The Edwards family, James Eisnor, Clarence Ernst, Jerry Fergusen, Mr. and Mrs. Chris Field, Rick Field, Julia Fillmore, Mr. and Mrs. John Frank, Bernie Gates, Janette Getson, Hugh Gough, Mr. and Mrs. Joseph Green, Amie C. Guyette, Virginia Guyette, Alan Haid, William R. Hall, Jr., Mort Hanson, Sr., Andrew Harvey, Mr. and Mrs. Lincoln Harvey, Rick Hebb, Garnett Heisler, Mrs. Louise Hersey, Mr. and Mrs. Carmen Hirtle, Art and Peggy Holland, Bruce Hopkins, Chris Huntington, Ellen Huntington, Mrs. Lloyd Hutt, Kieth Ingersoll, Bob Jackman, Mr. and Mrs. Frank Jardis, Mr. and Mrs. Laurie Jordan, Marshall Kaiser, Blair Kaizer, John Kidd, Paul Killowee, Ron Korman, Mr. and Mrs. Joe LaBeau, Edith Lamerock, Erving Langille, Wayne Leary, Donald Levy, Mr. and Mrs. Jesson Levy, Mr. and Mrs. Harry Levy, Mr. and Mrs. Kingsley Levy, Mr. and Mrs. Roy Levy, Frank and Toni Lillianthal, Blake Lynch, Norm Marple, John Matheson, Walter Meissner, Billy Mill, Daisey Mill, Hope Mill, Jabez Mill, Mr. and Mrs. Roy Mill, Al Minucci, Jack and Kathleen Mosher, The New Brunswick Museum, Mr. and Mrs. Doug Nickerson, Mrs. Fred Nickerson, Leslie Nickerson, Lloyd Oliver, Sam Pennington, Mr. and Mrs. Eugene Perry, Mr. and Mrs. Lloyd Perry, Mr. and Mrs. Harry Porter, Ralph and Patricia Price, Janet Rafuse, Mr. and Mrs. John Ramsay, Mr. and Mrs. Lewis Ramsay, Lloyd Ramsay, Ralph Ramsay, William Ramsay, Earl and Judy Rhodenizer, Jim and Mary Richards, Burton Robertson, Glenn Robertson, Marcia Ross, David Rowlings, Mr. and Mrs. Donald Rowlings, Amateur Savoie, Stanley Sawler, Mr. and Mrs. Vernon Schnare, Don and Nancy Scothorne, Mr. and Mrs. Cyril Selig, Doug and Elizabeth Selig, Norman Seymour, Mrs. Ruth Shapiro, Sandy Shapiro, Mr. and Mrs. Ron Sharp, Dan Slocum, Dr. and Mrs. Donald Southerland, Jamie Stalker, Robin Starr, David Stevens, Mr. and Mrs. Rudolph Stevens, Vincent Stevens, David and Debbie Stewart, Murry Stewart, Sam and Sally Stewart, Herb Stoddard, Don Stone, Mr. and Mrs. Richard Swaine, Paula Swenson, Forbes Tanner, Mr. and Mrs.

Russell Tanner, Jr., Mr. and Mrs. Solomon Tanner, Warrin Tanner, John and Kathy Turnbull, Hugh Valiant, John Weaver, Dennis White, Douglas White, Steven White, Mr. and Mrs. Preston Wilcox, Greg Willett, Mr. and Mrs. Bud Wilson, Lorne Wishart, Myles Wishart, Mrs. Alan Zwicker, and thanks also to those whose names we may have forgotten to include here.

Foreword

It is our intention in this book to establish the importance of the Canadian—Maritime Provinces, particularly Nova Scotia, Prince Edward Island, and New Brunswick, as centers of wildfowl carving worthy of attention by collectors of decoys. For too long, quality decoys carved by people from this region, have made their way to American or upper Canadian markets where they remain as unknowns or are mistakenly attributed to other carvers. The lack of any reference source on the area, the usually increased value of a decoy when sold as American made, and until recently, the too few native collectors all contributed to making identification difficult. In 1965 William F. Mackey, Jr. wrote in his book *American Bird Decoys,* "The Maritimes have added little to the history of decoys, and their makers for the most part, duplicate the efforts of carvers on the Maine coast. No one carver stands out from the field and except for the offhand, primitive examples a certain sameness exists in the rather heavy handed decoys of the region." It became obvious to us when we began buying Maritime Canadian decoys, that this quotation is exceedingly misreprensentative of the region. Yet for many years Mackey's book was the primary reference source on decoys and so his description prevailed. However, his book is not the only decoy book to deal inaccurately or unfairly with the area. Indeed, in all the decoy books that have been written in the past, most of them end their coverage of the decoys at the American-Canadian border as if the flyways ended there and so too the history of the decoy. It is time to give proper credit to the decoy carvers of Nova Scotia, Prince Edward Island and New Brunswick. We would like to make available for general reference, the information that we as collectors and dealers have succeeded in accumulating. We hope that those people who are unfamiliar with Maritime-Canadian decoys, as well as those who already share our appreciation of them, will use and enjoy the material on the following pages.

When we decided to write this book we had already collected a large number of decoys from the Maritimes and had saved what little information was available. But the more we became involved, the more misinformation about this area we encountered. With the help of those dealers, pickers and collectors who were willing to tell us where they found certain decoys (some were unwilling to reveal their sources) we began our detective work. Armed with a camera and stacks of photographs, with lists of names of gunners, of neighbors, of descendents, and most happily of the living carvers, we would roam the countryside and establish the facts as best we could. We toured fish shacks and barns, knocked many a random door, checked dates on tombstones when necessary, and cross checked our findings. But with this type of pioneer research where much of the information is old and difficult to confirm, it is perhaps inevitable that we have made some mistakes. We feel that it is important that corrections be made when such mistakes are found and would encourage one to do so.

The following photographs and text reflect the integrity of a wonderful heritage of carvers, who created not to satisfy a now flourishing decoy—art market, but to satisfy their own personal sense of what a wildfowl decoy should be. Some are beautiful; some are amusing; and some are simply examples of the make-do industry of a frugal people. The decoys illustrated are primarily working models, used to lure the wild bird and the vast majority are not less than thirty years old. Although there are some very fine decorative bird carvings and decoys being produced in the Maritimes today, only a few examples are included where we feel they are most appropriate in this work. It would also be impossible to include in this book, an example of every carver's work, especially of those in Nova Scotia where there are nearly as many people who carved decoys as there were people who hunted over them. We have tried to give a picture of the general styles that prevailed in various sections, to better enable others to identify a decoy with a region. It might also be mentioned that we were told about old time decoy carvers whose works were highly praised, but we were not able to find any examples of their work. Maybe, at some future time, with other decoy enthusiasts taking care to research and record information about the decoys they find, this work we have begun may be expanded to include those whom we are sorry to have missed.

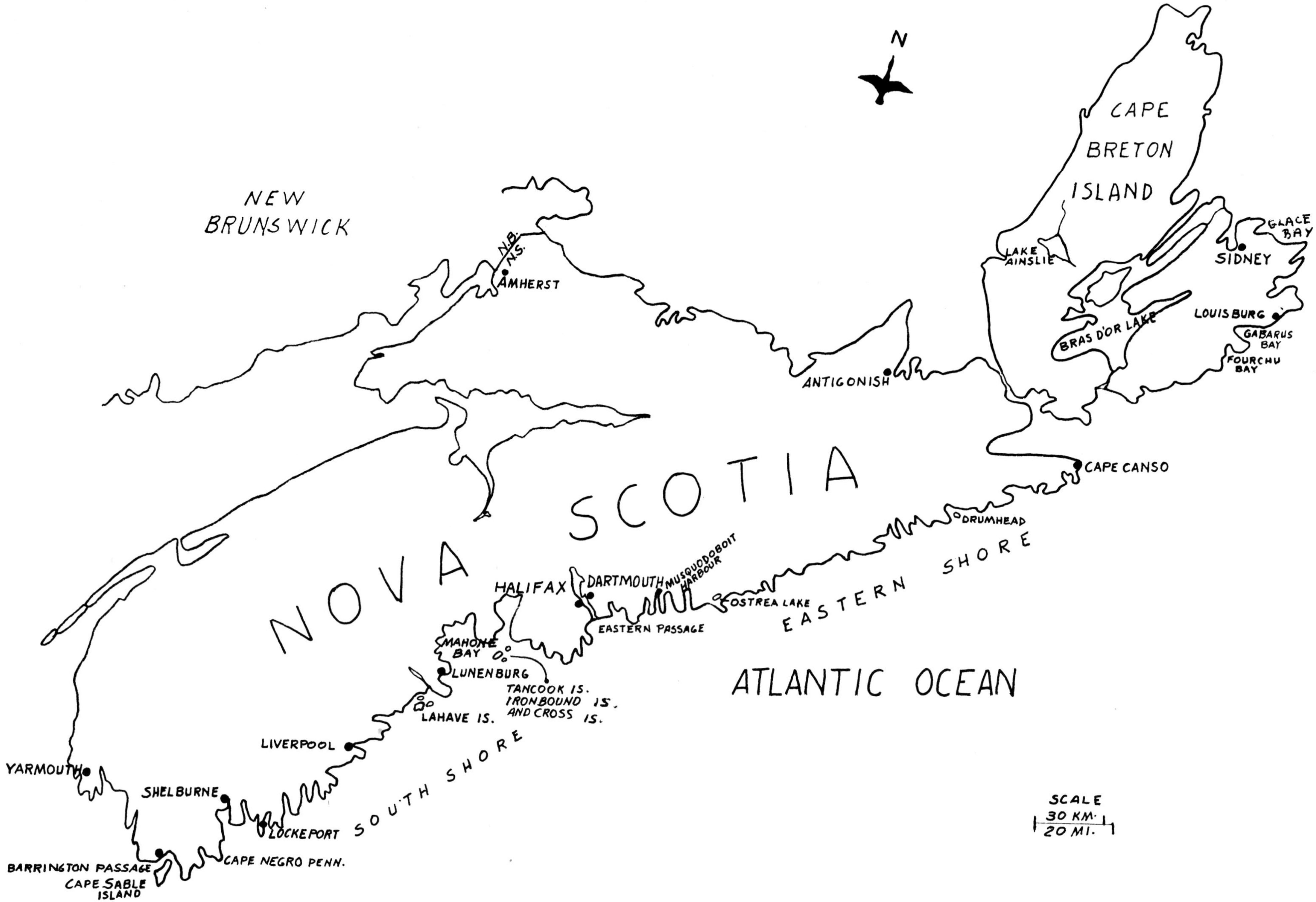
N
NEW BRUNSWICK
N.B.
N.S.
AMHERST
CAPE BRETON ISLAND
LAKE AINSLIE
BRAS D'OR LAKE
SIDNEY
GLACE BAY
LOUISBURG
GABARUS BAY
FOURCHU BAY
ANTIGONISH
CAPE CANSO
NOVA SCOTIA
DRUMHEAD
EASTERN SHORE
HALIFAX
DARTMOUTH
MUSQUODOBOIT HARBOUR
OSTREA LAKE
EASTERN PASSAGE
MAHONE BAY
LUNENBURG
TANCOOK IS.
IRONBOUND IS.
AND CROSS IS.
LAHAVE IS.
ATLANTIC OCEAN
LIVERPOOL
SOUTH SHORE
YARMOUTH
SHELBURNE
LOCKEPORT
CAPE NEGRO PENN.
BARRINGTON PASSAGE
CAPE SABLE ISLAND
SCALE
30 KM.
20 MI.

Part I

Nova Scotia

The story of the decoys of Nova Scotia is in a sense a continuation of the story of Atlantic Flyway decoys but until now very little accurate information was available on what has been produced there. Nevertheless, the diversity of style and intense creativity expressed in these decoys make it well worth taking a good clear look.

When we begin to delve into the history of Nova Scotian waterfowl decoys and their carvers it becomes necessarily a discussion of the people and their culture. Isolated geographically from the main body of Canada and the United States, we find a people traditionally preoccupied with the sea. By trade most carvers were fishermen, sailors, boatbuilders or lighthouse keepers. Fishing is a seasonal occupation however, and most of the other sea related occupations left time for the often favored past-time of carving or whittling. Most of the bird hunting was sea related also. Merganser, whistlers, loons and black-ducks could be hunted fairly close to the salt water shore although some could also be found inland on fresh water. Eiders, scoters and old squaws were in most cases found several miles out on the shoals and around the rocks where a person needed a boat and the know-how to use it to get near these areas.

For the most part, these people had little money to spare. They did not buy their decoys but instead made their own with the result being a great number of people who carved only a small number of birds each. There were few commercial carvers. However, there were some carvers who did sell decoys and it is interesting to note that a lot of the trade was with tourists and sportsmen from the United States. Many hundreds of decoys by various carvers left Nova Scotia in this way and yet few seem to have actually turned up in the States except those that have been brought there more recently as part of the antique-decoy market.

Loon from Fox Point on the Blandford Penninsula, Nova Scotia, circa 1900.

An assortment of merganser decoys from Lunenburg County, Nova Scotia.

Most of Nova Scotia's decoys are found along the Atlantic coast from Cape Sable Island in the south to Glace Bay in the north. The irregular coastline with its many sheltered bays and inlets is a perfect resting area for waterfowl. The remainder of Nova Scotia, including Cape Breton Island, has yielded little in terms of quantity or quality.

The section of coastline which runs northeast of Halifax is known as the Eastern Shore. To the south-west of Halifax the coast is known as the South Shore. The southern end of the South Shore from Lockeport to Barrington Passage was settled mainly by Loyalists from New England around the end of the American Revolution in the early 1780's. A large number of them were from Cape Cod and, in fact Shelburne was also called Cape Cod Colony. Many of the most common surnames in Shelburne and Barrington are the same as on Cape Cod. The land is poor for farming but fishing and ship-building were major industries. The most commonly hunted waterfowl along the South Shore are whistlers, eiders, scoters and some blackducks, bluebills and mergansers. The seaduck must have come in closer to shore around Shelburne and Barrington than in other areas because hunters were able to set out small rigs of about fourteen decoys and hide in the rocks nearby, ready to ambush the birds as they came in. Most of Nova Scotia's small numer of commercial carvers were in this area.

On the northeastern end of the South Shore is Lunenburg County, the most important area in Nova Scotian decoy history. It is probably the merganser decoys of mainland Lunenburg County which have gained the greatest notariety among decoy collectors in recent years and the many examples that have surfaced show distinct regional characteristics and have a certain special appeal. Although mergansers and merganser decoys are found elsewhere in Nova Scotia, there is no single area which produced so many nor with so much "folk" artistry. The live merganser is a bird which lends itself well to capturing the imagination of any carver. Lunenburg County, populated predominately by people of German descent, is well known among antique enthusiasts for appealing Germanic folk style paint and carving decoration on the early furniture and accessories made there. It is probable that this heritage of attention to artistic

Warren Tanner of Stonehurst, Nova Scotia still uses the gunning tub and seaduck rig that his father, Solomon made in 1924.

detail extended to the carving of decoys. It is possible also that more people in this area hunted mergansers for eating because German cuisine was more able to cover a usually rank tasting meat. However, time and time again, throughout Nova Scotia, we were told that many people did indeed eat (or sell for eating) not only mergansers, but also eiders, scoters and loons, the flesh of which is usually considered inedible in other areas. A likely reason for this may be simply that young birds killed early in the season do not taste as bad as later in the season when they are further south and older. Several old hunters recalled that even in the 1950's killed eider and loon were sold in the Tancook Island market for five cents and ten cents a pound. It is evident that it was not only the sport that motivated these people to hunt, but more importantly a way of putting food on the table.

Loon decoys, though not easy to find anywhere, are perhaps a little more common in Nova Scotia. Loons and mergansers were hunted in the more protected inner bays and river inlets. Hunters would use a single loon decoy but the usual rig of mergansers consisted of twelve to fourteen birds, about four of which were drakes and the rest hens. The red breasted merganser decoy is most often found but some common mergansers have turned up. Mahone Bay and Lunenburg Harbor are the two primary areas for these birds.

Way out in Mahone Bay, around the islands of Tancook, Little Tancook and Ironbound and off Cross Island there are large expanses of shoals and rocks where a great deal of hunting is done for eiders and scoters. The method used for hunting them requires skill and endurance. A few people today still use a gunning tub, a type of floating blind similar to the sinkbox but differing in several ways. The sinkbox was designed to hunt birds which came to feed near the shore in quite shallow water. The Nova Scotia gunning tub however is used primarily to hunt eider and scoter. The tub is deeper and a gunner generally squats or stands to shoot instead of lying down as in the sinkbox. It is used in areas that are miles from shore, where the water is quite deep and often rough. Large numbers of seaduck decoys (80 to 150) are arranged in a pattern on the water near the tub in a way meant to attract the live birds. Two dozen or so decoys are mounted on the wing board rim of the tub. It is a method of hunting seaducks extensively practiced by the hunters of these islands off the Lunenburg County coast. It is evidently quite effective and the only way to go after the birds in this area.

The construction of a decoy is related a great deal to how it is meant to be used, which in Nova Scotia is primarily on the sea. The eider decoys generally do not have the wide flipped up tails that are more characteristic of those decoys found in Maine. Instead they are distinguished by having tails that are square and narrow and stick straight out from the body. Some of the seaduck decoys show no tail at all. The tails on decoys from Little Tancook Island are further distinguished by being round on the bottom and across the end but flat on top. According to some of the older hunters this is an attempt to simulate the appearance of the young eiders who feed around the rocks. The evident result is that their tail feathers suffer much wear and tear and are often knocked off.

The eider decoy of Nova Scotia is usually a much used veteran of the hunt. The salt water wreks havoc on the paint so they must be repainted frequently. Consequently it is the exceptionally well cared for, or seldom used old eider decoy which does not have layers and layers of paint.

Along the Eastern Shore of Nova Scotia the carved decoys tend to be more crudely made but the decoys in general show great ingenuity on the part of the people who made them. The Mic Mac Indian influence is evident in the use of stick and seaweed decoys used for the hunting of geese. Silhouette or shadow decoys of geese, coot, scoter and snipe were commonly used. Full bodied stickups were sometimes made by stuffing canvas with seaweed or straw. We thought for a while that these were coot decoys but found out that they were used to hunt cormorant. Sometimes leather, folded and molded into a rough head shape would be mounted on a wooden body. Full bodied homemade tin decoys of geese and blackduck occasionally turn up and root head decoys of both geese and shore birds are more common in this area. Merganser decoy blocks may be finished by covering it entirely with the head and body skin and feathers of a killed bird, and goose decoys sometimes have dead goose wings tacked on. A common contrivance was the attachment of a small pile of seaweed to the back of a fully

Eider drake from Blue Rocks, Nova Scotia, circa 1890. This eider is from a large rig of seaducks. Seven decoys from this rig had open bills holding mussels. Most of them were quite damaged and only this one still retained the mussel.

fashioned and painted scoter decoy. Weights for the decoys could be had by simply using whatever was available and worked well, including doorknobs, rocks, door bolts, oxshoes and sparkplugs.

A sandbox method of hunting called a sink tub was used along the Eastern Shore. In order to make one, a hunter had to wait until the tide was out, and then would build a rock pile on the mud flat. A wooden box, that was narrow but was about four feet deep would be set on the pile and more rocks would be piled around it to anchor it in place. It was a permanent set-up and the exact site was often marked by a buoy, as the tub would be completely submerged at high tide. A hunter would wait until the top of his tub began to show as the tide went out. He'd then take a pail, bail it out and set his decoys up around the tub. He'd generally stay in the tub through the low tide and leave when the incoming high tide forced him out of it. Some people use a more complex type of sink tub which telescopes upward as the tide comes in, and therefore it can be used for a longer period of time.

The principle hunting areas of Cape Breton are St. Espirit, Fourchu Bay and Gabarus Bay along the Atlantic coast, and Bras D'Or Lake in the interior. Primarily blackduck, whistler, bluebill, and merganser can be found here. Some geese and seaduck are hunted, but there is much less interest today in seaduck hunting than there used to be. It seems that the whole art of decoy making died out in Cape Breton, unlike the rest of the maritimes where it still flourishes. Although using decoys to hunt waterfowl was a fairly strong practice in these parts, most of the old wooden decoys were burned or discarded many years ago and few people have tried their hand at making replacements.

In the last twenty years or so hunting birds has lost only a little of its intensity in Nova Scotia. The bird population is somewhat diminished but is strengthened by several wildlife sanctuaries, some of which protect waterfowl only. Most of the old carvers are no longer living. However, there is a renewed interest in carving in general, and some decoys and decorative bird carvings are now being produced.

Jesse Clayton Obed (1878-1932) was a fisherman and later a lighthouse keeper at the Half Moon Lighthouse. The lighthouse was located on a half moon shaped rock island, also called "The Salvages", off shore from the town of Blanche, Nova Scotia. It was while living and working at the lighthouse that Jess carved his decoys. Their graceful and realistic styling earned him the local title "King of the Decoy Carvers". Dozens of other carvers in the Cape Negro and Ingomar Peninsulas, including Everett "Happy" Hersey and Lloyd Perry were influenced to copy his style. Jesse's decoys all have glass eyes, fully carved bills and a very smooth finish. The whistlers have an indentation running horizontally through the eyes and some are hollow. The eiders all have inlet heads that are pegged to the body. About half of his eiders were hollow with a very thin board set in the bottom. Apparently he carved only twenty-four eiders (two rigs) but made several hundred whistlers. Jesse and Everett Hersey, his assistant at the lighthouse, used to hide in the rocks off the Half Moon and ambush seaducks and whistlers that they decoyed in.

Lloyd Perry (1917-   ), Jesse Obed's great grandnephew from Cape Negro, Nova Scotia, was assistant lighthouse keeper to Everett Hersey at the Half Moon ("The Salvages") lighthouse, and later, Everett's successor. In the 1940's, he began carving eider, scoter, and bluebill decoys. After a while his bluebills were repainted as coots. He was definitely influenced by Jess and Everett in his decoy styling but added a little of his own variation. His scoters are large and have inlet heads. His eiders have heads in Obed's style but they are connected to the body with a false inlet (a Tancook characteristic) and the bodies have a distinctly Tancook style tail. Lloyd spent some time on Tancook Island and decided that he preferred the flat, squared off tail style used there to Jess and Everett's flip tail.

Everett (Happy) Hersey (1898-1975) of Blanche, Nova Scotia, worked as Jess Obed's assistant on the Half Moon Lighthouse from 1917 until 1932 when Jess died. Everett then continued running the lighthouse until 1945 when the system became automated. It was during his years working with Jess that Everett began carving his decoys although he continued carving for many years afterwards. His style of decoy is strikingly similar to Jesse's.

Everett made many full-bodied eiders and whistlers and scoter shadow decoys for his own use and for his friends. He used a hatchet to rough them out of cedar blocks and brought them to a smooth finish by scraping them with a piece of glass. Everett also made gun stocks and gun parts.

Warren Perry (1912-), a fisherman from Cape Negro, Nova Scotia, hunted with Jess Obed and Everett Hersey. He carved eider decoys in the 1940's that were hollow and very similar to Obed's, but they are a little cruder and have a blocky tail. Warren Perry's initials are usually carved on the underside of his decoys.

Fred Nickerson and son carving scoter decoys, circa 1935.

Fred Nickerson (1902-1980) was born in Villagedale, Nova Scotia. He lived in the United States periodically for thirty-one years where he worked as a boatbuilder and an inspector for the U.S. Navy in Massachusetts, Rhode Island, New York and Maine. He carved his extremely fine working decoys in both Massachusetts and Nova Scotia in the 1930's. In the late 1970's he made decorative bird carvings while living in Florida. Fred carved bluebills, whistlers, scoters and eiders, but his finest work was done on his merganser decoys. The mergansers have horse hair crests and carved wings with the white wing markings outlined with an incised line. The paint work is fairly simple but carefully done with pleasing muted colors. Some whistler decoys were carved jointly with his hunting buddies Frank Lamerock and Ken Coffin. Fred's best work was his earlier decoys. His later carved birds are not quite as skillfully made.

Fred started the Western Shelburne County Fish and Game Association in Barrington Passage, Nova Scotia. It later developed into the Beaver Dam Shelburne Sports Association Incorporated.

Frank Lamerock (1907-1977) was a carpenter from Reynoldscroft on the western shore of the Cape Negro penninsula. He regularly hunted on Barrington Bay with the Perry brothers, but his principle hunting partners were Fred Nickerson, Ken Coffin and Stan "Goose" Lamerock. He carved whistlers, mergansers and eiders which he sold for one dollar apiece. Later on he carved decorative birds including flying mergansers and miniatures. One fall, Frank, Ken Coffin and Fred Nickerson jointly carved thirty-six whistlers of which they kept one dozen each for their own use.

Noble Stewart (1929-), a fisherman from the north side of Cape Sable Island, carved about two hundred whistler, bluebill and seaduck decoys to sell during the 1950's and 60's. His folky style is a more refined version of his father Ken Stewart's work.

Ken Stewart (1891-1969), a fisherman, was one of the principal commerical carvers on Cape Sable Island during the first half of the twentieth century. He carved between four and five hundred decoys, most of which were whistlers.

Romie Leslie Swim (1905-1973) was a carver from Clark's Harbor on Cape Sable Island. Between 1920 and 1960, he made whistler, bluebill and blackduck decoys to sell and for his own use. He also made duck heads which he sold. In the late 1950's, he made around ten flying drake whistlers for his own rig. These flying decoys were used as floaters with the tails weighted down so that the heads would be angled out of the water.

Enos Perry (1879-1975) was a commercial decoy carver and fisherman who lived in Northeast Harbor, Nova Scotia. He was born in Ingomar and moved to Northeast Harbor in the early 1900's, but his principle hunting partners, John and Fred Doan, and Alex Perry, were all from

Ingomar. Enos carved around two thousand eider, scoter, whistler, old squaw, and merganser decoys in his simple but functional style. In his later years he carved miniature decoys as gifts for his grandchildren and friends.

Doug Nickerson (1898-   ) was born in Port Latour, Nova Scotia. He lived for fourty-seven years in the United States however before moving back to Nova Scotia in the early 1950's. His home in Cape Negro was right next door to Lloyd Perry. He began carving in the 1950's upon his return to Nova Scotia. He made eiders, whistlers, blackducks, bluebills and geese; about two hundred in all. His decoys have glass eyes and bulging cheeks. His blackducks are hollow but the rest of his decoys are solid.

Oscar Crowell (1917-   ) from Smithville, Nova Scotia, on the Cape Negro peninsula, carved and used most of his decoys in the 1930's. He then moved to Ontario where his seaduck decoys were of no use. The fifty or so eider, scoters, and young scoter decoys were stored for the next fourty years. In 1974, Oscar and his wife Beryl moved back to Smithville where he rerigged some of his decoys and began hunting with them again. He also carved another batch of decoys to add to his rig at this time.

Crowell's decoys are skillfully made and have a very lifelike appearance. They have glass eyes, raised wings, carved bills and small notched tails. Carved in a horseshoe shape on the underside of the tail of his decoys, is his name.

Bruce Hopkins (1949-   ), Oscar Crowell's son-in-law, was also from Smithville. He made an almost identicle version of Oscar's decoys. The tails however, are somewhat smaller and the undersides are of course not stamped with Crowell's name. For both Oscar and Bruce, each decoy took four days to make.

John Smith (1882-1968), from Barrington, Nova Scotia, was the most prolific of the Nova Scotian decoy carvers. Over a period of seventy years, he carved and sold between three and four thousand whistler, bluebill, blackduck and eider decoys. He also made some decorative bird carvings, and occasionally painted decoys for other people. The majority of his decoys were whistlers and bluebills since the primary hunting in his area was in the back bays. Smith's own regular shooting area was off Throes Island which is nestled way up in the protective bay formed between the Cape Negro peninsula and Cape Sable Island. Today many of his decoys are still in use in the Barrington — Cape Sable area, but they have also regularly turned up all the way from Yarmouth to Liverpool.

Smith's mass production of decoys didn't leave much time for detailed carving or elaborate styling. His birds have painted eyes, little or no neck and very simple but adequate bodies. The paint is quite detailed but primitively done. There are a fair number of Smith copies made by other carvers, some of which are painted by Smith himself.

Roy Penny (1933-   ), a "Jack of all trades" from the region called South Side on Cape Sable Island, has carved and sold between seven and eight hundred working black duck, scoter, eider and mallard decoys. Today he carves and sells decorative loons, swans, and gulls. Most of his working decoys have applied wings with raised crossed tips, made out of cedar shingles and tacked to body.

Willard Robertson (1884-1970), from Osbourne Harbor, was the principal decoy carver in the Lockeport, Nova Scotia area. Although he sold few decoys, he carved many rigs as gifts for friends and acquaintances. He made blackducks, whistlers, and bluebills as working decoys, and mallards as full size mantel birds. He also carved miniatures.

Until 1961, Willard was a master carpenter and cabinet maker for the Lockeport Company, a division of National Sea Products. He used Joel Barber's book *"Wild Fowl Decoys"* for acquiring the patterns for his decoys. Using illustrations from this book he carved whistlers and bluebills in the manner of Benjamin Holmes and Albert Laing, two well known Stratford, Connecticut carvers, as well as his own regular style. He also made a few decoys which are quite similar to decoys that he owned by Billy Ellis of Whitby, Ontario.

Frank Selig (1878-1953), the grandson of celebrated Captain Adam Selig, was a fisherman from Voglers Cove, Nova Scotia. Frank made a large rig of hollow blackduck decoys and a couple of seagull confidence decoys for duck hunting on the calm waters of Medway Harbor. His favorite spots were near Smiths and Selig Islands. The blackduck decoys, with their sleek body lines, swept up tails, and high cocked back heads, have excellent sculptural form. Selig also made solid body whistler decoys. An extremely active big game and duck hunter, Frank used a smokehouse in his back yard to keep his family well supplied with smoked salmon, mackeral, deer, moose and smoked duck.

Burns Williams (1906-1981) lived just outside of Lockeport, Nova Scotia. He carved around three hundred working blackduck, whistler and bluebill decoys in the 1930's through the 1960's. When he retired from his job at the Lockeport fish plant in 1972 he began carving decorative birds and miniatures to sell to tourists and antique pickers. His decoys have glass eyes, bold but simple paint patterns and fairly short necks. Some of his earlier blackducks are hollow.

Captain Edwin Backman (1872-1914) carved the most stylish of the Lunenburg County decoys. Unfortunately he carved very few, fourteen mergansers and perhaps twenty five whistlers and scoters. Unlike other really good carvers it seems he had very little influence on the carvers around him, the only exception being a rig of six somewhat cruder whistler decoys turned up at a son's residence. Backman's decoys are characterized by strong flowing lines and muted color. The mergansers have long delicate bills which protrude cone-like from the head. The crests are wooden and thin and start somewhat far forward on the head. The drake mergansers have particularly intricate paint.

Captain Backman was an off-shore fisherman and captain of a cargo schooner which worked out of Lunenburg, Nova Scotia. In his work he traveled extensively to Newfoundland, Europe and the West Indies. At the outbreak of World War I he set sail in his three masted schooner, the "William Cortada", for the West Indies and was never heard from again. Backman felt his schooner was poorly designed, and before leaving, he confided to his friends and family that his new schooner would "be the death of me".

Alexander (Sandy) Levy (1864-1927), was a fisherman from Little Tancook Island. His self-sufficient life style included many fall and winter days of seaduck hunting with his Saxon ten gauge shotgun. Sandy and his father, **George Levy** (1843-1926), carved hundreds of eider, scoter, merganser, and old squaw decoys from about 1875 to 1925. They made their own large rigs plus many more to sell or trade with fishermen on both Tancook and Little Tancook Islands. They seem to be the creators of the Tancook tail; flat topped with a rounded bottom and end. Both George and Sandy's birds show whittle marks and a false inlet of the head to the body. Many are found with square nails holding the weights on the bottom. George's decoys tended to have shorter bodies than Sandy's, and a distinct champher around the bottom edge.

Lindsey Levy (1892-1980) of Little Tancook Island, began carving with his father Sandy and grandfather George about 1910. His father's and grandfather's influence on his carving style can be seen in Lindsey's earlier decoys but he soon developed a much more flowing body and head style including changing their design of the tail. His decoys have more carefully applied paint and don't show the whittle marks like theirs do. Lindsey's later birds often had glass eyes. They also had the lead weights inserted in hollowed out keels. This was done to protect the decoys from being marked by the lead weights when they were piled on top of each other. Many of his decoys were made for selling or trading.

William Raymond Levy (1912-1971), a neighbor and distant relative of Lindsey Levy on Little Tancook Island, borrowed decoys from Lindsey in order to begin carving his own. However, he kept, and even further exaggerated the Tancook style tail on his decoys. His birds either have no eyes or painted eyes. He made scoters, eiders, whistlers, mergansers, old squaw and two loons.

Rudolph Stevens (1939-   ) was born and raised on Tancook Island. He worked as a boatbuilder until 1969 when he began working on the ferry which runs between the mainland and Little Tancook Island, Tancook Island and Ironbound Island. He carved a large rig of blackduck decoys for his own use which are feather painted and have half inch holes drilled into the bottoms to make them float higher in the water. The earlier ones tend to be hollow instead of having drilled holes. He also made several full bodied stick-up seagull decoys to set on the shore near his blind. Rudolph carved about one hundred fifty blackduck, old squaw, eider and scoter decoys from the mid 1950's to 1972. Most of the blackducks were carved jointly with Robert Langille.

Harry Levy (1910-), Lindsey Levy's nephew, was born on Little Tancook Island. He moved to Lunenburg in 1946 but still used the Tancook style tail when he began carving blackducks and eiders in the 1950's. He painted his decoys with special care and attention to detail. In particular, the finely blended paint on the heads of his earlier blackducks is among the best paint work to be found in Nova Scotia. Harry still carves working decoys today as well as decorated swordfish swords.

Manson Young (1883-1953) lived on big Tancook Island where he worked as a fisherman and farmer. He made the usual Tancook assortment of seaducks, old-squaw, blackducks, whistlers, mergansers and a couple of loons. Manson spent a lot of time on Ironbound Island and left many of his decoys there.

Kingsley Levy (1908-), nephew of Manson Young, worked most of his life as a fisherman off Little Tancook Island. Between 1920 and 1970 he carved about two hundred seaduck, whistler, merganser, blackduck and old squaw decoys and one loon. At 74 years of age, he still used a gunning tub and a full seaduck rig to hunt with. A large number of the scoter decoys in his rig were carved by **Albert Levy** (1901-1928), also from Little Tancook Island.

Milford Levy (1895-1972), from Little Tancook Island, Nova Scotia, was a fisherman who carved a rig of over two hundred eider and scoter decoys for his own use. Like most seaduck decoys from the Tancook area, Milford's had the heads pegged onto the bodies. He also made many back preeners and open mouthed seaducks.

Vincent Stevens (1915-), a carver from big Tancook Island, made about seventy-five eider, scoter, old squaw, whistler, and merganser decoys during the 1930's and 40's. Most of these decoys were lost on Mahone Bay while he was hunting with them at different times. A carpenter and fisherman until his retirement, Vincent then made full rigged schooner and yacht models.

Another carver from big Tancook Island was **Harvey Cross** (1895-1981). A fisherman by trade, Harvey made between one and two hundred eider, scoter, merganser, and old squaw decoys in his spare time. His hunting partner was his brother Ralph who also shared in some of the carving.

Solomon Tanner (1894-) worked as a fisherman out of Stonehurst, Nova Scotia. In the winter of 1924, Solomon, with the help of his brother Jessen, cut down a very large pine tree and, on sleds dragged it across the ice to his home. From this one tree they made about one hundred fifty eider and scoter decoys and two gunning tubs. Solomon would anchor his tub about three miles out in the ocean, a journey which would take between one and two hours, depending on how much ice he had to break through. Although Solomon no longer goes seaduck hunting, his son Warren still uses the tub and decoys that his father made.

Dennis White (1899-) lived in Stonehurst, Nova Scotia, until the early 1950's, at which time he moved to Lunenburg. Like most men in Stonehurst in the early 1900's, he worked as an inshore fisherman and lobsterman. Dennis began making his whistler decoys in the 1920's. He carved approximately five hundred of them over the next thirty years, both for his own use and for selling. Many of his simple but functional decoys are still in use around Lunenburg and Mahone Bay. In the 1950's, Dennis carved miniature whistler decoys that with their doweled on heads, carved eyes and squared off tails, are exact miniature versions of his working models.

Steven White (1912-), a fish culler and boat plant worker from Lunenburg, carved about two hundred fifty bluebill, whistler and seaduck decoys between 1930 and 1970. Most of his decoys were for his own use but he also carved a few to sell. When Steven was growing up in Eastern Point, south of Stonehurst, he spent a lot of time fishing and hunting with men from Ironbound Island and made his seaduck decoys with their styling techniques. Steven's whistler and bluebill decoys are plump, with well rounded heads, and have raised wing outlines that lay over the tail.

Douglas White (1910-) was born in Eastern Point, Nova Scotia, but moved to Bayport in 1920. Although he worked all his life as an inshore fisherman, in the 1930's he began carving blackduck, bluebill, whistler, and seaduck decoys to sell. He still carves today and his total output so far is between five and six hundred decoys. Douglas's decoys are similar to his brother Steven's but are larger and more elaborately carved.

Gilbert Rafuse (1908-) lived in Gold River, Nova Scotia until 1947 when he moved up the shore to Chester Basin. A master carpenter by trade, his wood working skill is also evident in the design and execution of the decoys he has made. He carved several rigs of whistlers and mergansers and a few old squaw. Guilbert's 1980's decoy models are very similar to the ones that he made in the 1930's and 40's.

Cecil Swimer (1928-) an inshore fisherman from Gold River, Nova Scotia, used to hunt regularly with Blair Kaizer. He carved a small rig of mergansers and whistlers to use while hunting along the inner shores of Mahone Bay. They all have applied, notched tails made from cedar shingles.

Russell Tanner Sr. (1911-1979) was one of the better known carvers in the fishing village of Stonehurst, Nova Scotia. Russell was a fisherman who began carving old squaw, bluebill whistler, blackduck and merganser decoys in the early 1940's. He also made full rigged ship models, one of which is on display in the Lunenburg Museum.

Another Lunenburg carver who used the Tancook tail on his decoys was **Guilford Bezanson** (1893-1960). He carved several hundred bluebills, blackducks and whistlers for his own use and for selling to hunters and tourists from the United States. Guilford began carving in the 1930's but he made most of his decoys in the 1950's, after he retired from fishing. He also made flying duck whirly-gigs and half-size decoys.

Irving Tumblin (1892-1976) was a hunter and trapper who lived on Wolf Island in the LaHave Island group. He carved blackducks, old squaw and mergansers, mostly for his own use. His blackducks were made with the burn and scrape method more common in New Brunswick than Nova Scotia. They were quite large with thin beaks and high necks. His drake mergansers had wooden crests. The hen mergansers had no crests but many are found with hair crests that were added at some later time. His later model mergansers had shoe eyelets for eyes. When he wanted to hunt scoters he coated his blackduck decoys with stove blackener which could be washed off when he wanted to switch back to hunting blackducks.

John Stanley Sawler (1887-1966) from the town of Western Shore on Mahone Bay, hunted, trapped and worked as a guide in the area. He carved several hundred mergansers and whistlers and at least one loon, for his own use and for selling. His merganser decoys originally had leather crests although many were altered to wooden crests or horse hair crests. The pattern of paint on the wings of his merganser decoys is outlined in pencil.

Blair Kaizer (1912-) of Gold River, Nova Scotia, started hunting at twelve years of age. He quickly became a well known duck hunter. In the 1930's Stan Sawler made a merganser for him which he used as a model to carve a rig for his own use. Blair began using killed birds for models for other merganser decoys and about a dozen blackduck decoys. He also carved bluebills, whistlers, and one seagull. His blackduck decoys are distinguished by the paint on the heads. They are entirely covered with dots which were applied with a pointed stick. Blair did not

Blair Kaizer with his hunting gear in 1980.

carve a great many birds but those he did carve are appealing and well made.

Percy Shupe (1877-1962), from the town of Western Shore on Mahone Bay was one of the earlier Mahone Bay carvers. He began carving in the mid 1890's when he worked on "Captain Ryan's sealing ship". At this time he made decoys for himself and for his friends. They would be out sealing for the entire winter, during which time Percy developed into a crack shot. It is said he could regularly shoot the cork out of a brandy bottle thrown from the ship.

In the 1920's he worked as a guide and began carving sets of decoys (three hens and one drake) to use on his hunting expeditions. He made about one hundred merganser sets, quite a few whistlers and about a half dozen black ducks. He sold most of these decoys to local gunners and to hunters from the United States who hired him as their guide. Percy's mergansers all had fringed leather crests, racey styling typical of the Lunenburg County area, and somewhat protruding cheeks. His whistler decoys have raised wings, protruding breast and big cheeks. Percy also repaired other people's decoys and often put heads he carved on other decoy bodies. During this time he learned that he had tuberculosis and wasn't expected to live very long. He began taking one tablespoon of seal oil two times a day and lived another fifty years.

Percy worked on the fishing banks with Orran Hiltz and Clarence Ernst during the 1930's and 1940's and even though he was supposed to have been very secretive about his decoy patterns, both Clarence and Orran's carving greatly resembles Percy's original patterns.

Orran Hiltz (1901-1978) from Indian Point, is one of the most well known of the Nova Scotian decoy carvers, probably because the early discovery and distinct Lunenburg County styling of his work brought him quick but deserved notariety.

One of his merganser decoys is illustrated in Starr's *Decoys of the Atlantic Flyway,* page 209. Orran carved between four and five hundred seaduck, whistler and merganser decoys, and in the 1970's carved many miniature mergansers. His earlier decoys have raised wings and flipped up tails, a form possibly obtained from Percy Shupe. His mergansers have wooden crests. In the late 1950's he simplified his decoys by eliminating the raised wings and lowering the tail.

Clarence Ernst (1912-) is one of the many Indian Point hunters who copied Orran Hiltz's styling. His birds are somewhat cruder however, and his merganser decoys sometimes have leather crests. His whistlers are styled like Percy Shupe's whistler decoys but are slightly larger and less refined. Clarence started carving about 1950 since which time he made about fifty decoys.

Otis Hatt (1871-1946) from Chester Basin, Nova Scotia, carved what could be described as typical Lunenburg County style merganser decoys. They had racey lines, leather crests and fairly simple paint. A cooper by trade, he carved decoys in his spare time for his own use and some for sale. He also made miniature whistler carvings, some of which he gave to his children to play with.

Ned Mackay (apx. 1905-1978) was a fisherman from Little Harbor, which is located in the center of the Eastern Shore, Nova Scotia. He carved several hundred decoys for selling and for his own use, many of which were made with his brother John. He didn't make any birds after about 1955. His merganser decoys can be identified by the large heads and very elongated wooden crests on the drakes. He also made whistler, eider, old squaw and scoter decoys all of which have a sharply ridged tail and a pegged and wedged on head. His black ducks however are made of cork with wooden heads. The whistler decoys he made can be identified by their exaggerated pointed heads and sharp protruding cheeks.

Carroll Gardiner (1918-) from Dartmouth, Nova Scotia, made decoys which have been found in many places along the Eastern Shore. His favorite rig of merganser decoys was stolen from his hunting camp so he began stamping his initials "CRG" in the center of the back of his birds. Carroll's decoys are fairly flat bodied with heads that are pegged on and then wedged in the peg. He carved scoters, eiders, mergansers and whistlers.

Clyde Edwards (1899-1976), a fisherman from Eastern Passage, Nova Scotia, carved some bullhead plover and golden plover which were thrown away years ago. He also carved forty-six old squaw, thirty-six blackducks, twenty-four blue bills, twenty-four scoters and one oversize seagull. Most of these fine decoys are hollow, and except for the blackducks, are repainted several times. They all have glass eyes and are quite realistically styled.

Alfred P. Murphy (1887-1972) was a fisherman from Murphy's Cove. He carved eiders, mergansers, whistlers, coots and scoters, mainly for his own use. His decoys had a high flipped tail and the eyes were placed very high on the head.

Marshall Kaiser (1899-) was born in Port Bickerton on the Eastern Shore of Nova Scotia where he carved working decoys. In 1920 he moved to Sidney on Cape Breton Island and set up a locksmithing business. While living and hunting in Cape Breton, he carved over one thousand blackduck, whistler, bluebill, merganser and seaduck decoys. Primarily his decoys were blackducks for use in the many sheltered bays and inlets on Bras D'Or Lake. Most of Marshall's decoys have inletted heads with a screw through the center to give them strength. More recently Marshall's interest shifted to making full rigged schooner models.

Robert F. Baker (1906-), an inshore fisherman from Clam Harbor, Nova Scotia, carved approximately three hundred eiders, scoters, old squaw, whistlers, teal, blackduck and merganser decoys. His birds have fairly smooth lines for the Eastern Shore, and the heads are pegged onto the bodies with the peg showing through the top of the head. Robert's son, Foster Baker, has carved decoys that are simpler versions of his father's.

William Rowlings (1891-1962), ex-postmaster of Musquodoboit Harbor, and decorated World War I veteran, was also the most well known decoy carver in that area. He was an avid waterfowler who made decoys for his own use as well as many to sell. He carved several hundred eider, scoter, and whistler decoys, all of which have the typical Eastern Shore turtle back styling and pegged on heads. Rowlings made between fifty and sixty roothead yellowlegs and rock plover, and several rigs of stick (or cane) geese. Although a few other carvers along the Atlantic coast of Nova Scotia made shorebird decoys, Rowlings' shorebirds are the only ones that we know to have surfaced.

Daniel Stevens (1905-1973), a fisherman from Owl's Head, Nova Scotia, made whistler, eider and scoter decoys. He carved from 1935 to 1970, and made decoys for selling as well as for himself.

Captain Leonard Williams (1883-1967), from Ostrea Lake, Nova Scotia, worked out of Halifax as captain of a schooner which hauled coal and lumber to New York City. During World War I, he commanded a minesweeper in the Canadian Navy. After World War I, he captained small freighters and served again in World War II.

Ostrea Lake is one of the few areas in Nova Scotia where goose decoys turn up in quantity, and many of them are stick (or cane) goose decoys which were carved by Leonard Williams. He also carved a large rig of seaduck decoys.

Harold Burke (1888-1970) of Drumhead, Nova Scotia, on the Eastern Shore, is most well known for his wide, flat eider decoys. With their carved bills and flowing, almost flounder-like body lines they are appealing examples of decoy folk art. Harold also made many blackduck, scoter, merganser, old squaw and whistler decoys.

Harold grew up living in Drumhead Lighthouse where his father was the lightkeeper. He ran the light briefly himself before moving ashore and taking up a career of inshore fishing. His four brothers and several other hunters in the area made seaduck decoys which were similar to Harold's but most of them lack the flair that Harold's work has.

Wellington Rafuse (1904-1982) was a professional hunter, trapper and fisherman from Fourchu on the southern shore of Cape Breton. He was an interesting character and well known to the fishermen and hunters along the whole southern shore. He is pictured and written about in the booklet *Images of Canada.*

Wellington carved several hundred seaducks, blackducks, mergansers, and old squaw for his large and much used gunning rigs. A year or so before his death, Wellington's gunning tub and most of his decoys were burned as obsolete.

Erving Langille (1932-   ), a fisherman from Louisburg in Cape Breton, lived on big Tancook Island until 1952. He made a large rig of hollow blackducks that are very similar to the decoys of carver Douglas White who was a friend of his when he hunted on Mahone Bay. Erving also carved a rig of hollow goose decoys but used composition heads and necks. When he moved to Louisburg he took a rig of bluebill and whistler decoys with him that were made by Guilford Bezanson, who was carving and selling decoys in Lunenburg at the time.

Eider hen and drake by Jesse Clayton Obed, Blanche, Nova Scotia, circa 1910. This particular pair of Obed eiders are solid bodied but several others from the same rig were hollowed out with a wooden plate inserted in the bottom.

Whistler hen and drake by Jesse Clayton Obed, Blanche, Nova Scotia, circa 1920. Obed carved several hundred of these whistlers, some of which were hollowed out with an inset plate and others which were left solid.

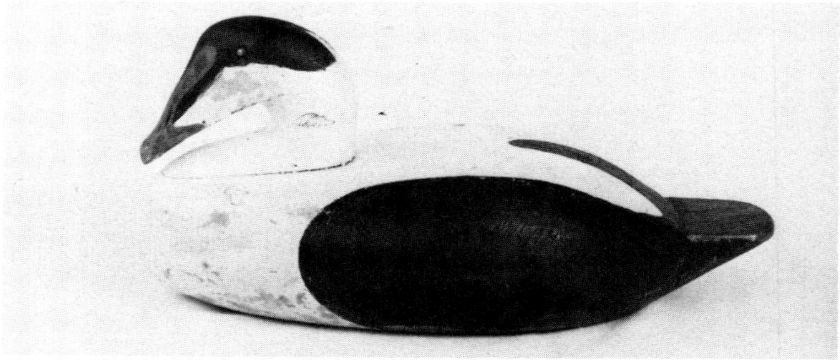

Eider drake by Lloyd Perry, Cape Negro, Nova Scotia. This decoy shows strong Obed influence in the head and breast but it also has a distinctly Tancook style tail.

White winged scoter by Lloyd Perry, Cape Negro, Nova Scotia. The head is inlet to the body.

Eider hen and drake by Allen Ross, Stoney Island, Nova Scotia.

Bluebill repainted as a coot by Lloyd Perry, Cape Negro, Nova Scotia. The original work and the repaint are both Lloyd Perry's work.

Eider hen by Everett Hersey, Blanche, Nova Scotia, circa 1920. This decoy was carved while Hersey was Obed's assistant at the Half Moon Lighthouse and shows strong Obed influence including an inlet head.

Whistler hen by Everett Hersey, Blanche, Nova Scotia, circa 1920. Very similar to Jesse Obed's work.

Eider drake by Warren Perry, Cape Negro, Nova Scotia, circa 1940. Hollow, strong Obed influence.

Eider drake, Obed influence. This hollow decoy was found hanging in an outhouse in Southwest Port Mouton. With it were three others by the same carver and one Jesse Obed eider. Carver unknown.

Half size whistler hen (white face markings are a latter addition), by Fred Nickerson, Villagedale, Nova Scotia, circa 1930.

Old squaw drake from the Lockeport area, circa 1900.

Whistler hen and drake by Al Doan, Gunning Cove, Nova Scotia, circa 1900.

Flying merganser drake by Frank Lamerock, Reynoldscroft, Nova Scotia, circa 1955.

Whistler hen and drake by Frank Lamerock, Reynoldscroft, Nova Scotia, circa 1900. The wings of many of Lamerock's decoys are carved in relief, as they are on this pair.

Eider drake,Frank Lamerock, Reynolds-croft, Nova Scotia, circa 1948.

Eider hen and drake by Noble Stewart, Cape Sable Island, Nova Scotia. Shows some Obed influence.

Whistler hen by Noble Stewart, Cape Sable Island, Nova Scotia, circa 1955. Shows the influence of ***Frank Lamerock.***

Whistler drake by Ken Stewart, Cape Sable Island, Nova Scotia, circa 1925.

Eider hen by unknown carver. Jesse Obed influence.

Whistler drake by Enos Perry, Northeast Harbor, Nova Scotia, circa 1940.

Eider drake and hollow blackduck by Doug Nickerson, Cape Negro, Nova Scotia, circa 1950.

Eider hen by Oscar Crowell, Smithville, Nova Scotia, circa 1932. Notched tail. Signed O.L. Crowell.

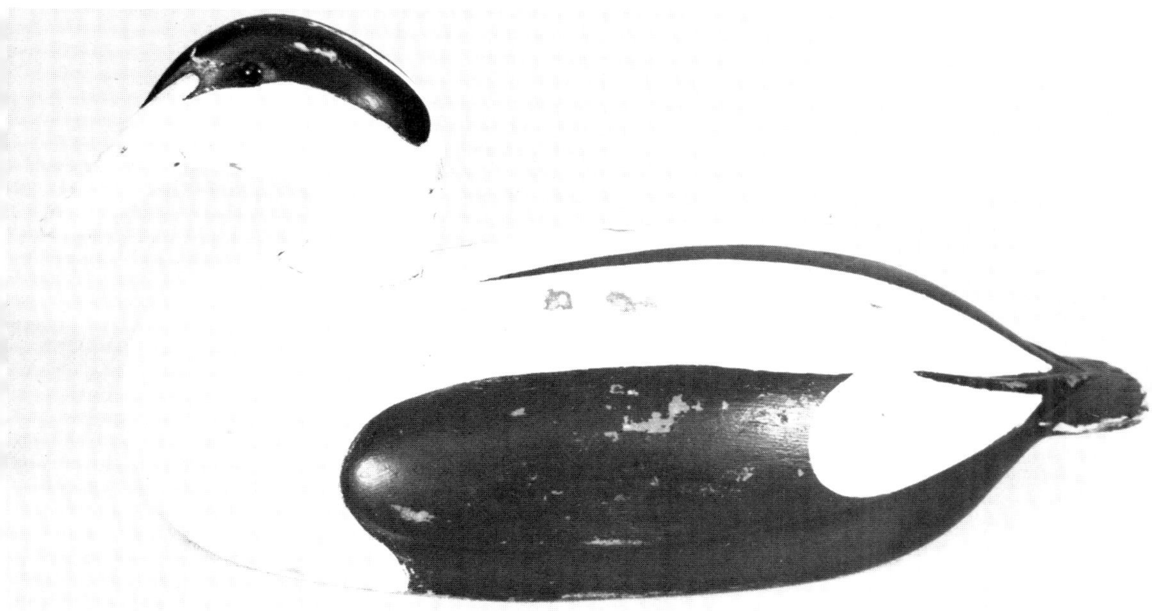

Eider drake by Oscar Crowell, Smithville, Nova Scotia, circa 1932. Notched tail. Signed O.L. Crowell.

Whistler hen by Oscar Crowell, Smithville, Nova Scotia, circa 1940's. This decoy is one of many mass produced by Crowell when he lived in Ontario. It is made of plastic which was poured into a mold that Crowell designed. The paint work is by Crowell's hand.

Eider hen by Bruce Hopkins, Smithville, Nova Scotia. Hopkin's decoys greatly resemble his father-in-law, Oscar Crowell's work except that the tails on Hopkins birds are not notched, and are smaller. Also the heads tend to be smaller.

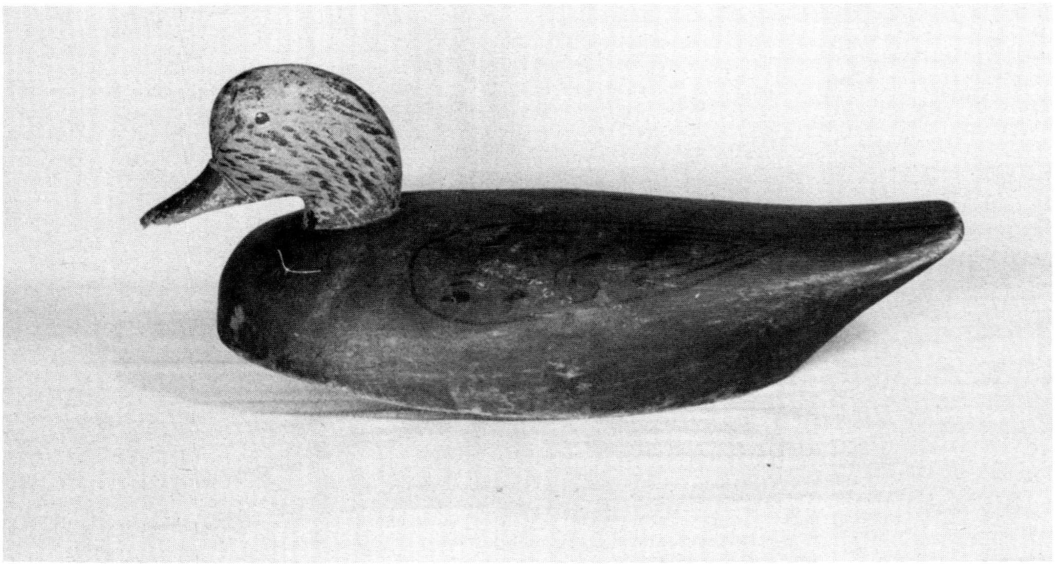

Blackduck by John Smith, Barrington, Nova Scotia, circa 1930.

Bluebill hen by John Smith, Barrington, Nova Scotia, circa 1960.

Whistler hen by John Smith, Barrington, Nova Scotia, circa 1920.

Eider drake by Bruce Hopkins, Smithville, Nova Scotia.

Eider drake and hen by John Smith, Barrington, Nova Scotia, circa 1925.

Whistler drake and bluebill drake by John Smith, Barrington, Nova Scotia, circa 1920. Because of the quantity of decoys made and the consistancy of his style, Smith is probably the most readily recognized decoy carver in Nova Scotia.

Seagull by John Smith, Barrington, Nova Scotia.

Eider hen and drake by Roosevelt Penny, Cape Sable Island, Nova Scotia, circa 1955.

Scoter decoy by Roosevelt Penny, Cape Sable Island, Nova Scotia, circa 1950. Penny's decoys have applied wings made out of cedar shingles tacked to the body.

Eider hen by Roosevelt Penny, Cape Sable Island, Nova Scotia.

Merganser drake by Earl Messenger, Barrington, Nova Scotia, circa 1925. Painted by John Smith.

Loon decoy with inlet head by unknown carver, Sandy Point, Nova Scotia, circa 1910.

Bufflehead hen and drake by Gus Nickerson, Cape Sable Island, Nova Scotia.

Flying whistler by Romie L. Swim, Clark's Harbor, Nova Scotia, circa 1950. This decoy had lead weights under the tail so when floating in the water the head would be angled up as if it were taking off.

Pair of mallard miniatures and full size whistler hen by Willard Robertson, Osbourne Harbor, Nova Scotia. These are examples of Robertson's later work, circa 1955.

Blackduck, found on the south shore of Nova Scotia. Head is constructed of a core of wood with string wrapped around it and painted.

Harlequin duck, one unknown decoy maker's version of a very unusual decoy, Cape Sable Island, circa 1900.

Whistler hen by Willard Robertson, Osbourne Harbor, Nova Scotia, circa 1910.

Whistler drake and blackduck by Willard Robertson, Osbourne Harbor, Nova Scotia, circa 1940. Robertson probably acquired the form for these birds from some other decoys in his rig which were carved by Billy Ellis of Whitby, Ontario. The paint is Robertson's own.

Whistler hen and drake by Willard Robertson, Osbourne Harbor, Nova Scotia, circa 1940. Robertson found pictures of decoys carved by Ben Holmes of Stratford, Connecticut, in Joel Barber's book, "Wild Fowl Decoys", from which he acquired the form for these decoys. The paint pattern is Robertson's own.

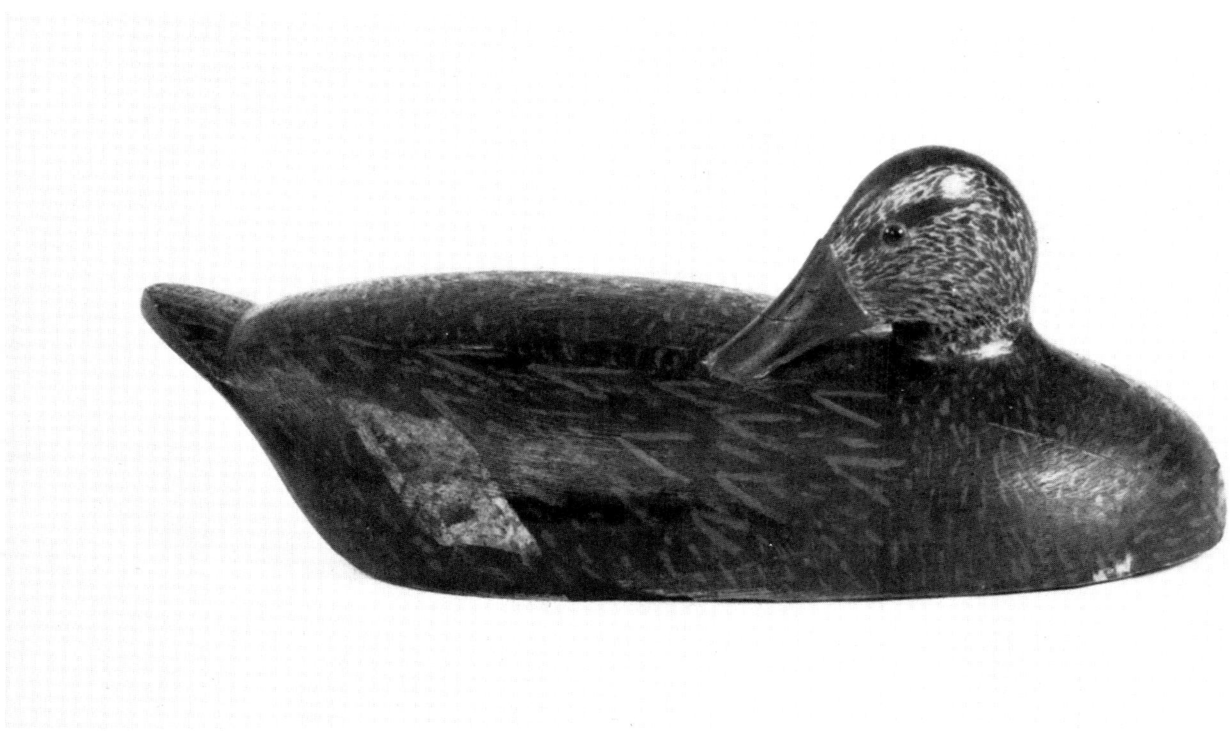

Preening blackduck by Burns Williams, Lockeport, Nova Scotia, circa 1940.

Blackduck by Burns Williams, Lockeport, Nova Scotia, circa 1930. This over painted decoy is one of Williams' earlier hollow models.

Whistler drake from the Lockeport area, Nova Scotia, circa 1930.

Seagull by Frank Selig, Voglers Cove, Nova Scotia, circa 1910.

Blackduck from Lockeport, Nova Scotia, circa 1930. The unknown carver of this streamlined decoy stamped the entire surface of the bird to give it a textured feathered appearance.

Whistler hen and drake, found in Lockeport, Nova Scotia. Copied from Mason Decoy Factory's standard or challenge grade decoys.

Merganser hen from Lunenburg, Nova Scotia. The head of this decoy is made by Edwin Backman and was probably mounted by him on an earlier merganser body that he found.

Whistler drake purchased from the Backman family, Lunenburg, Nova Scotia, circa 1930. Some stylistic similarities to known Edwin Backman decoys but definitely carved by another hand.

Old squaw drake by William Raymond Levy, Little Tancook Island, Nova Scotia, circa 1935.

Old squaw drake by Lindsey Levy, Little Tancook Island, Nova Scotia, circa 1920.

Old squaw drake by Sandy Levy, circa 1900 and old squaw hen by George Levy, circa 1880. Both of Little Tancook Island, Nova Scotia.

Whistler hen and drake by Sandy Levy, Little Tancook Island, Nova Scotia, circa 1890.

Eider hen and drake by W. Raymond Levy, Little Tancook Island, circa 1940. This pair of decoys was part of a large rig found near Blandford.

Two scoters by Milford Levy, Little Tancook Island, Nova Scotia, circa 1925. The open billed scoter originally held a mussel where now only the nail remains.

Bluebill hen and drake by Sandy Levy, Little Tancook Island, Nova Scotia, circa 1890.

Merganser hen by Sandy Levy, Little Tancook Island, Nova Scotia, circa 1890.

Merganser hen and drake by George Levy, Little Tancook Island, Nova Scotia, circa 1880.

Merganser drake by William Raymond Levy, Little Tancook Island, Nova Scotia, circa 1938.

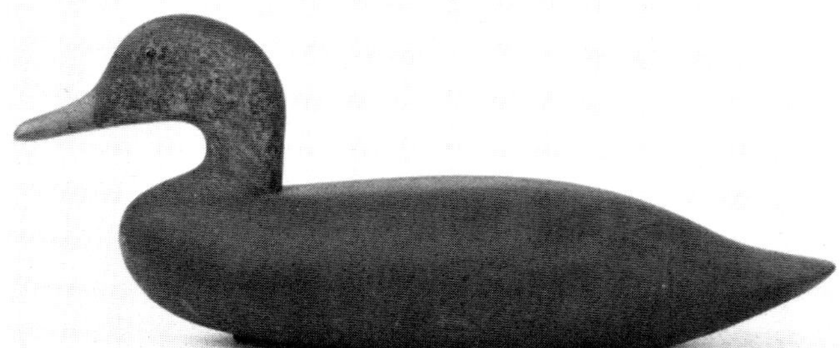

Blackduck by Lindsey Levy, Little Tancook Island, Nova Scotia, circa 1930.

Merganser hen and drake by Roy Levy, Little Tancook Island, Nova Scotia.

Loon by W. Raymond Levy, Little Tancook Island, circa 1940.

Scoter and unfinished decoy, probably a whistler, by W. Raymond Levy, Little Tancook Island, circa 1940.

Whistler hen and drake by W. Raymond Levy, Little Tancook Island, circa 1940. Raymond exaggerated the typical Tancook style tail on his decoys.

Eider hen, drake and juvenile hen by Kingsley Levy, Little Tancook Island, Nova Scotia, circa 1940.

Preening eider hen from Little Tancook Island, Nova Scotia, probably by Kingsley Levy, circa 1930.

Yellow bill scoter by Albert Levy, circa 1925 and patch bill scoter by Kingsley Levy, circa 1930, both of Little Tancook Island, Nova Scotia. Kingsley Levy's rig.

Preening scoter by Kingsley Levy, Little Tancook Island, Nova Scotia.

In late October, hunters on Little Tancook Island, Nova Scotia, get out their gunning tubs and rigs of seaducks in preparation for the seasons shooting. Kingsley Levy's rig of decoys is shown here with a view of Little Tancook Harbor in the background.

Seagull by Rudolph Stevens, Tancook Island, Nova Scotia, circa 1955.

Blackduck by Rudolph Stevens, Tancook Island, Nova Scotia, circa 1965. Half inch holes drilled into the bottom for buoyancy.

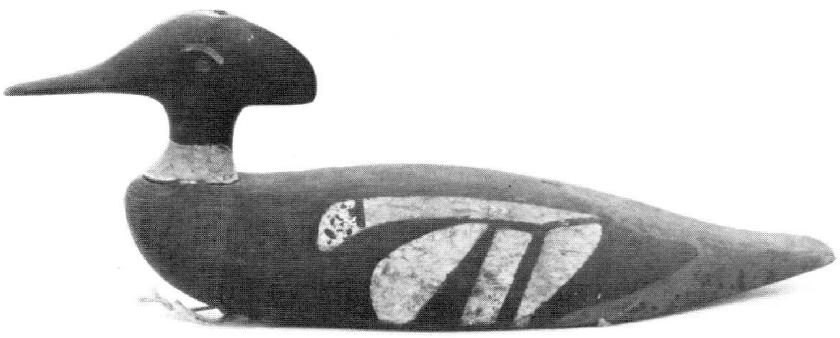

Merganser drake by Manson Young, Tancook Island, Nova Scotia, circa 1910.

Merganser hen by Manson Young, Tancook Island, Nova Scotia, circa 1910.

Loon by Manson Young, Tancook Island, Nova Scotia, circa 1910.

Merganser drake by Harvey Cross, Tancook Island, Nova Scotia, circa 1940.

Blackduck by Rudolph Stevens, Tancook Island, Nova Scotia, circa 1955. Hollow with wooden plate tacked onto the bottom.

Loon by unknown carver from Tancook Island, circa 1910.

Merganser drake from Tancook Island, Nova Scotia, circa 1900. Although the name Redford Sleunwhite is written on the bottom of this decoy, it was probably made by Redford's father, David Sleunwhite (1864-1938).

Merganser hen and drake by Vincent Stevens, Tancook Island, Nova Scotia, circa 1935.

Loon, Tancook Island, circa 1950.

Merganser hen and drake, found in Lunenburg, circa 1920. Strong Tancook Island characteristics are evident.

Old squaw drake from Liverpool, Nova Scotia. The tail feathers are made out of a dowel inserted onto the tail base.

Scoters from the Blandford Penninsula, Nova Scotia, circa 1940.

Blue bill from the South shore of Nova Scotia, circa 1930.

A hunter's shot box with Germanic design carved in the top; from the South shore of Nova Scotia, circa 1930.

Preening eider drake by Solomon Tanner, Stonehurst, Nova Scotia, circa 1924. Used as a wing duck on his gunning tub.

Whistler hen and drake by Dennis White, Stonehurst, Nova Scotia, circa 1930.

Whistler hen and drake by Steven White, Lunenburg, Nova Scotia.

Bluebill hen and drake by Steven White, Lunenburg, Nova Scotia, circa 1945.

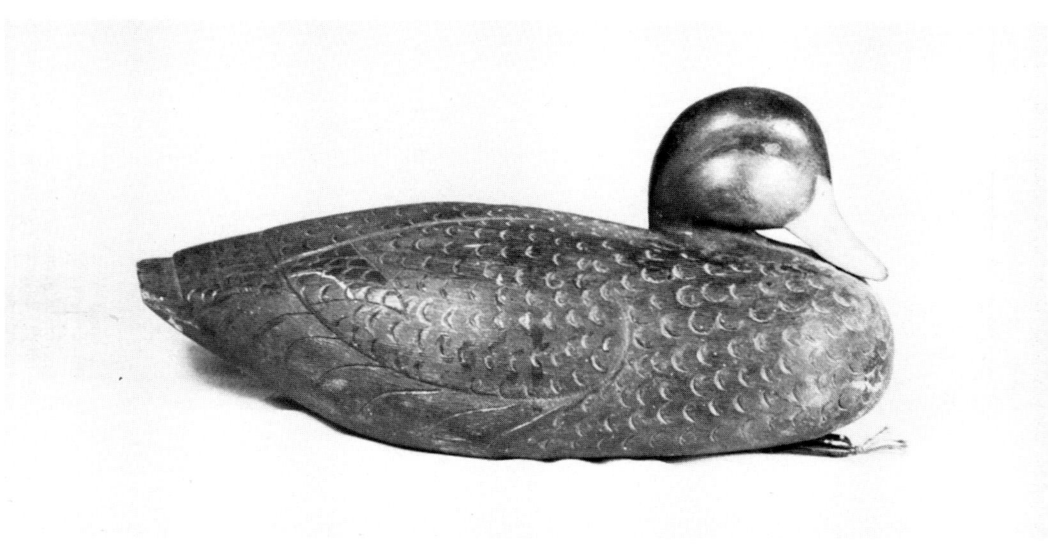

Blackduck by Douglas White, Bayport, Nova Scotia, circa 1950.

Blackduck from Feltzen South, Nova Scotia, circa 1930. This decoy is hollowed out and seamed through the middle.

Merganser drake by Gilbert Rafuse, Chester Basin, Nova Scotia, circa 1980. During the 1930's and 40's, Gilbert carved several rigs of mergansers that were very similar to his current work.

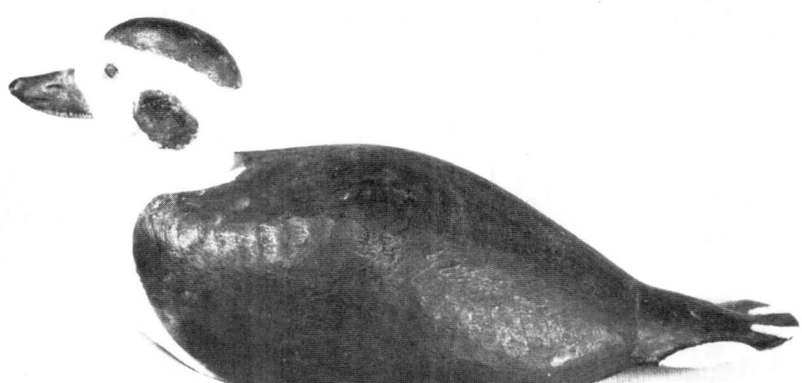

Old squaw hen by Gilbert Rafuse, Chester Basin, Nova Scotia, circa 1935.

Whistler drake by Cecil Swimer, Gold River, Nova Scotia, circa 1950. The notched tail is made out of an applied piece of cedar shingle.

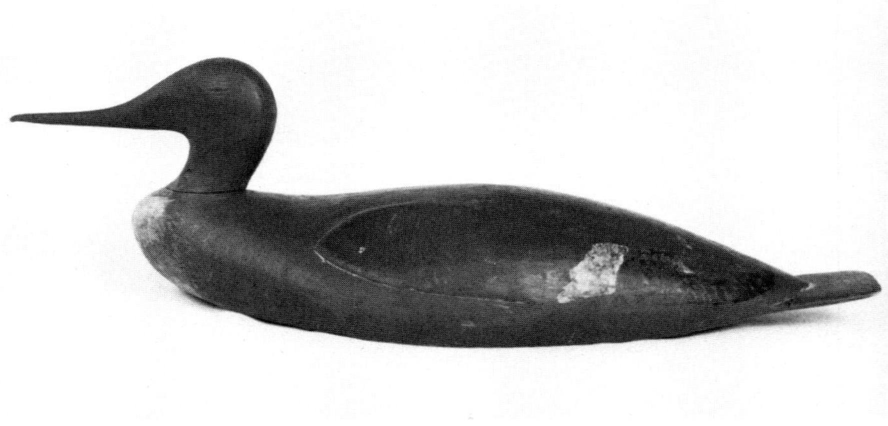

Merganser hen by Cecil Swimer, Gold River, Nova Scotia, circa 1950.

Merganser drake from Stonehurst, Nova Scotia, circa 1940. Forbes, Billy and Earl Tanner together carved about a dozen of these mergansers one fall, as well as about thirty eider decoys.

Eider hen with inlet head from Rose Bay, Nova Scotia, circa 1920.

Eider hen and drake from Blandford, Nova Scotia, circa 1920. The necks of these decoys are inlet to the bodies and secured with pegs. Large pegs protruding from the underside of the bodies enabled them to be mounted on the wing boards of a gunning tub.

Eider hen, circa 1930 and eider drake, circa 1950, by Russell Tanner, Stonehurst, Nova Scotia.

Whistler hen and drake by Russell Tanner, Stonehurst, Nova Scotia, circa 1950.

Stonehurst Harbor, Nova Scotia.

Eider drake from Kingsburg, Lunenburg County, Nova Scotia, circa 1900.

Blackduck by Russell Tanner, Stonehurst, Nova Scotia, circa 1950.

Whistler hen and drake from Lunenburg, Nova Scotia. Large square cut hole in the undersides.

Whistler hen from Lunenburg, Nova Scotia, circa 1930.

Oversized blackduck by Guilford Bezanson, Lunenburg, Nova Scotia, circa 1930.

Whistler hen and drake by Guilford Bezanson, Lunenburg, Nova Scotia, circa 1950.

Old squaw from Mahone Bay, Nova Scotia.

Merganser drake by J. Stanley Sawler, Western Shore, Nova Scotia, circa 1920. Sawler's earlier merganser decoys such as this were more streamlined and had a ridged backbone line.

Merganser hen and drake by J. Stanley Sawler, Western Shore, Nova Scotia, circa 1940.

Blackduck by Blair Kaizer, Gold River, Nova Scotia, circa 1935.

Whistler hen and drake by J. Stanley Sawler, Western Shore, Nova Scotia, circa 1940.

Merganser drake by Blair Kaizer, Gold River, Nova Scotia, circa 1935.

Mrs. Frances G. Byers' recipe for merganser

Take fresh plucked bird and wash the fuzz off under hot water. Soak the carcass overnight in cold water. Boil it for 1½ to 2 hours, changing the water three times. Drain and dry. Put an onion and half a small apple inside the cavity. Season inside cavity with summer savory, salt and pepper. Attach a strip of salt pork across the top with toothpicks. Cook for one hour in 325 ⁰ oven.

Old squaw hen from the south shore of Nova Scotia, circa 1910.

Seagull by Blair Kaizer, Gold River, Nova Scotia.

Merganser hen by Blair Kaizer, Gold River, Nova Scotia, circa 1930.

Whistler hen and drake by Blair Kaizer, Gold River, Nova Scotia, circa 1935.

Patchbill scoter by Oscar Crowell, Smithville, Nova Scotia, circa 1932.

Juvenile scoter drake by Oscar Crowell, Smithville, Nova Scotia, circa 1932.

White winged scoter by Oscar Crowell, Smithville, Nova Scotia, circa 1932.

Hollow blackducks by Frank Selig, Vogler's Cove, Nova Scotia, circa 1920.

Merganser hen by Orran Hiltz, Indian Point, Nova Scotia, circa 1940. A good example of his middle phase carving style. (Lillianthal Studio)

Brant from New London Bay, Prince Edward Island, circa 1900. (Lillianthal Studio)

Sleeping blackduck by Amateur Savoie, Neguac, New Brunswick, circa 1937. (Lillianthal Studio)

Golden plover by Havelock Mill, Mill's Point, Prince Edward Island, 1880. Branded HM *on the undersides. (Lillianthal Studio)*

Red breasted merganser drake by Captain Edwin Backman, Lunenburg, Nova Scotia, circa 1900. (Lillianthal Studio)

Whistlers by Captain Edwin Backman, Lunenburg, Nova Scotia, circa 1900. (Lillianthal Studio)

Loon by Lindsey Levy, Little Tancook Island, Nova Scotia, circa 1925. (Hebb's Photography)

Merganser hen and drake by Lindsey Levy, Little Tancook Island, Nova Scotia, circa 1940. (Hebb's Photography)

Scoter by Sandy Levy, Little Tancook Island, Nova Scotia, circa 1890. (Hebb's Photography)

Old squaw hen and drake by Lindsey Levy, Little Tancook Island, Nova Scotia, circa 1930. (Hebb's Photography)

Blackduck from Liverpool, Nova Scotia, circa 1920. (Lillianthal Studio)

Merganser drake from Mahone Bay, circa 1910. Crest is made of leather. (Lillianthal Studio)

Eider drake and juvenile by Jim Zwicker, Castalia, Grand Manan Island, New Brunswick, circa 1900. (Lillianthal Studio)

Golden plover, probably by John Ramsay, Summerside, Prince Edward Island, circa 1900.

Red breasted merganser drake by Fred Nickerson, Reynoldscroft, Nova Scotia, circa 1932. This decoy was found near his family home in Nova Scotia. (Lillianthal Studio)

Loon with inlet head from Sandy Point, Shelburne County, Nova Scotia, circa 1920. (Lillianthal Studio)

Bluebill hen and drake by Willard Robertson, Osbourne Harbor, Nova Scotia, circa 1930. (Lillianthal Studio)

Mallard hen and drake by Willard Robertson, Osbourne Harbor, Nova Scotia, circa 1940. Robertson made only a very few of these full-sized mantel birds in addition to hundreds of working decoys. (Hebb's Photography.

Bluebill hen and drake from the Lunenburg area of Nova Scotia, circa 1920. The heads are inlet to the bodies and they have Tancook Island style tails. Maker unknown. (Hebb's Photography)

Eider hen and drake by Jesse Clayton Obed, Cape Negro, Nova Scotia, circa 1920. The inlet heads and down-east form of these decoys are a good example of how some Maritime-Canadian decoys might easily be mistaken for having been carved elsewhere. (Lillianthal Studio)

Old squaw from Lunenburg County, Nova Scotia, circa 1920. Carver unknown.

Blackduck by Harry Levy, Lunenburg, Nova Scotia, circa 1945. (Lillianthal Studio)

Curlew and yellowlegs, attributed to Abram Thomas, Lennox Island Indian Reserve, Prince Edward Island, circa 1910.

Canada goose on ice platform by John Ramsay, Summerside, Prince Edward Island, circa 1890.

Merganser hen and drake found in Torrence Bay, Nova Scotia, circa 1900. This sleek pair of mergansers may well have been carved by Edwin Backman. The strong similarities with his known work are made questionable only by the particularly notable difference of tail design. (Lillianthal Studio)

Seagull from Lennox Island, Prince Edward Island, circa 1900. This hollow, oversized decoy is pictured with a Mason Factory dove decoy in order to show the relative size.

Blackducks by Blair Kaizer, Gold River, Nova Scotia, circa 1935. Blair used a small pointed stick to apply the dotted paint pattern to the heads. (Hebb's Photography)

Canada goose on ice platform by John Brooks, Freeland, Prince Edward Island, circa 1915. From his own hunting rig. (Lillianthal Studio)

Merganser hen and drake by Irving Tumblin, Wolf Island, Nova Scotia, circa 1930. (Lillianthal Studio)

Merganser hen and drake by Percy Shupe, Western Shore, Nova Scotia, circa 1900. Both decoys are old overpaints covering original primary coats of brown paint. The hen originally had a small leather piece tacked on for a tail.

Whistler hen by Percy Shupe, Western Shore, Nova Scotia, circa 1910. Old overpaint by an unknown hand.

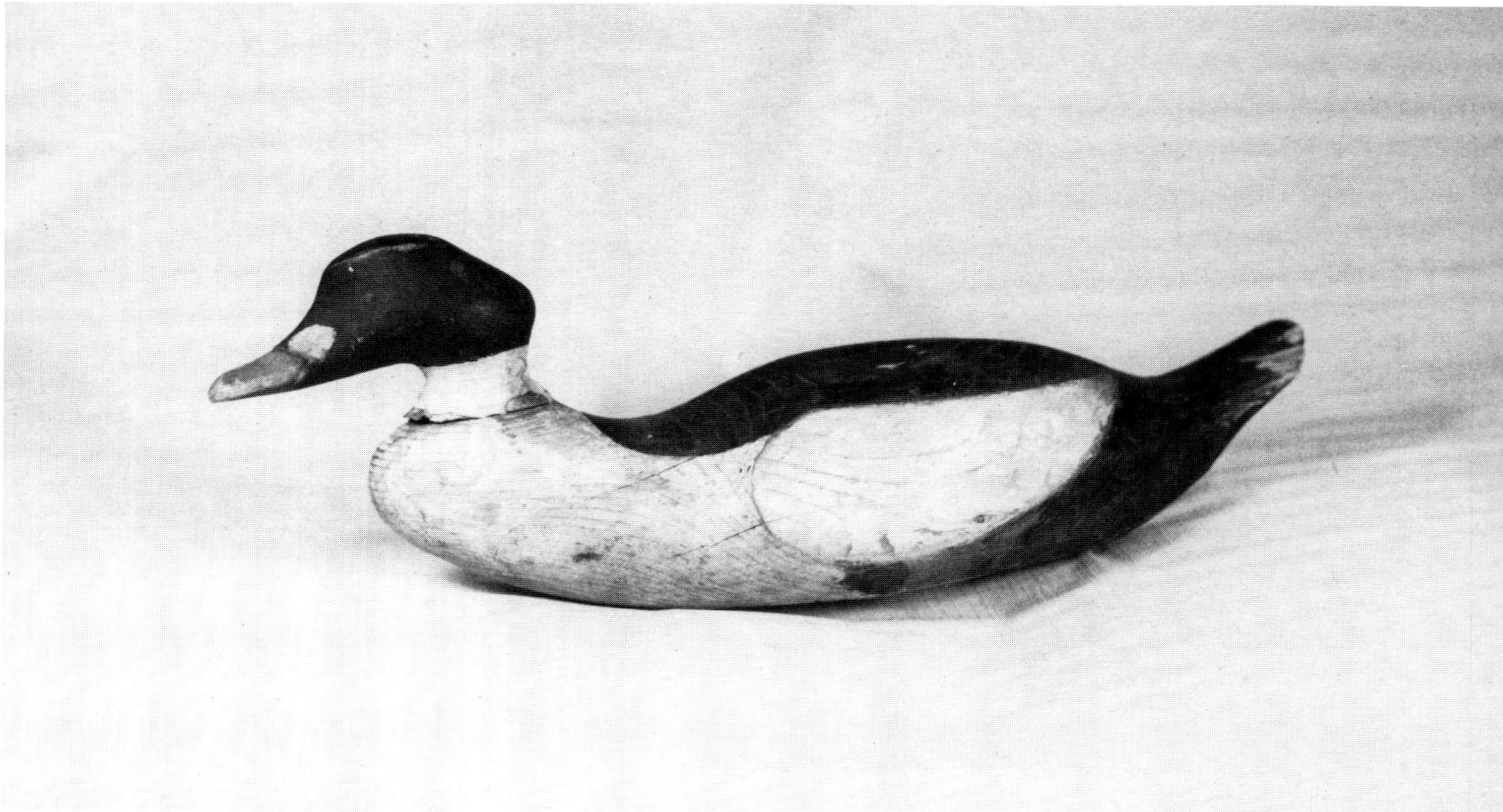

Whistler drake by Orran Hiltz, Indian Point, Nova Scotia, circa 1930.

Merganser hen and drake by Orran Hiltz, Indian Point, Nova Scotia, circa 1925. The hen may have originally been intended to be used as a drake since other merganser hens from this period of Hiltz's work do not have the scalloping on the crest. Strong similarities to Percy Shupe's decoys.

Merganser hen and drake by Orran Hiltz, Indian Point, Nova Scotia, circa 1960. A style change from his earlier work.

Whistler hen and drake by Clarence Ernst, Indian Point, Nova Scotia, circa 1940.

Merganser hen by Clarence Ernst, Indian Point, Nova Scotia, circa 1960.

Merganser hen and drake by Clarence Ernst, Indian Point, Nova Scotia, circa 1955. Ernst's copy of Orran Hiltz middle style.

Merganser hen by Otis Hatt, Chester Basin, Nova Scotia, circa 1900. Typical style of merganser found in the inner Mahone Bay region.

Merganser hen found floating on Mahone Bay by Blair Kaizer and Cecil Swimer. They shot at this bird several times before they realized it was actually a decoy.

Blackduck by Clyde Edwards, Eastern Passage, Nova Scotia, circa 1930. Because of certain styling characteristics, this decoy might easily be mistaken as being of Ontario origin. It is hollow and has a thick plate applied to the bottom.

Whistler hen and drake by Clyde Edwards, Eastern Passage, Nova Scotia, circa 1935.

Old squaw hen and drake by Clyde Edwards, Eastern Passage, Nova Scotia, circa 1935. Solid bodied.

Scoter by Clyde Edwards, Eastern Passage, Nove Scotia, circa 1930. Hollow with an applied wooden plate.

Bluebill hen and drake by Clyde Edwards, Eastern Passage, Nova Scotia, circa 1935.

Scoter and eider drake by Alfred Murphy, Murphy's Cove, Nova Scotia, circa 1930. Recently repainted by his son Leigh.

Blackducks by Marshall Kaiser, Sidney, Nova Scotia, circa 1925.

Whistler hen by Marshall Kaiser, Sidney, Nova Scotia, circa 1930.

Marshall Kaiser and friend returning from a morning's shooting, circa 1950.

Yellowlegs by William Rowlings, Musquodiboit Harbor, Nova Scotia, circa 1925.

Plover by William Rowlings, Musquodoboit Harbor, Nova Scotia, circa 1925. All of Rowlings shorebird decoys have pine branch heads.

Eider drake by William Rowlings, Musquodoboit Harbor, Nova Scotia, circa 1925.

Merganser hen by William Rowlings, Musquodoboit Harbor, Nova Scotia, circa 1920.

Merganser hen and drake by Robert Baker, Clam Harbor, Nova Scotia, circa 1940.

Scoter by Robert Baker, Clam Harbor, Nova Scotia, circa 1930.

Harlequin duck by George May, Musquodiboit Harbor, circa 1880. A very early and unusual decoy.

Canada goose from the Ostrea Lake region, circa 1930. Quite a few of these goose decoys with the roothead construction have surfaced in this area.

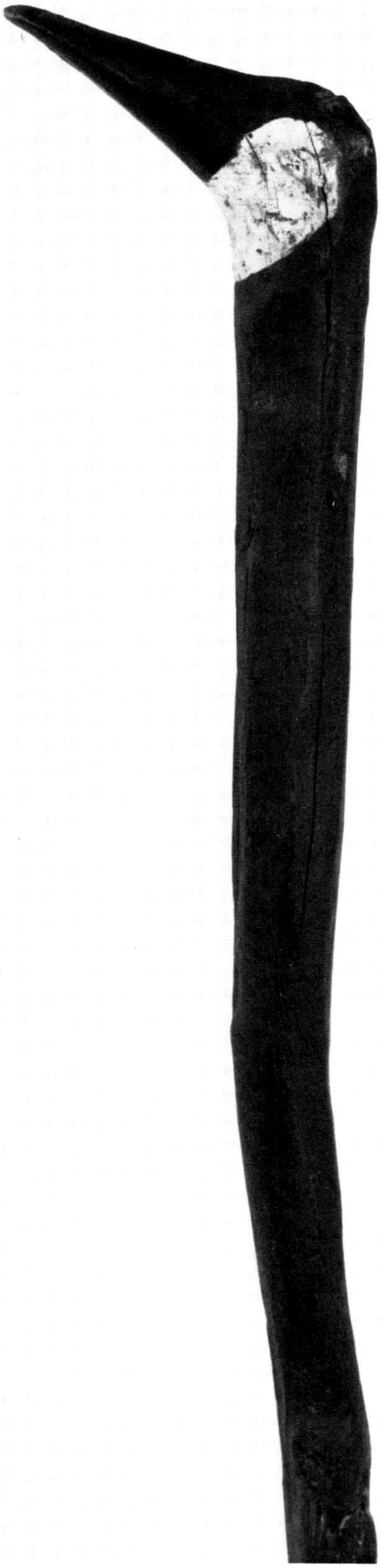

Goose stick decoy by Captain Leonard Williams, Ostrea Lake, Nova Scotia, circa 1930.

Seagull from the Musquodiboit Harbor region, circa 1930's. This decoy is hollow with an inset wooden plate on the bottom.

Eider drake from the eastern shore of Nova Scotia, circa 1940. This decoy is hollowed through the center and filled with lead.

Whistler hen and drake by Dan Stevens, Owls Head, Nova Scotia, circa 1950.

Eider hen and drake by Leslie Burt, Spryback Bay, Nova Scotia, circa 1930. This bob-tailed type of eider decoy is characteristic of many Nova Scotian eider decoys.

Whistler drake and scoter from Musquodoboit, Nova Scotia, circa 1925. Hundreds of decoys by this unidentified carver have been found scattered throughout the lower eastern shore of Nova Scotia.

Miniature eider drake and two whistler drakes found near Clam Harbor, Nova Scotia, circa 1945.

Merganser hen and drake, rigged next to each other on a pole, from the eastern shore of Nova Scotia, circa 1935.

Scoter from Head of Jedore, circa 1930. Seaweed is attached to the back of this decoy probably to suggest feathers.

Loon, from the eastern shore of Nova Scotia.

Eider drake by Harold Burke, Drumhead, Nova Scotia, circa 1930.

Eider drake and scoter found in Country Harbor, Nova Scotia, circa 1935. The eider is hollow with a thin wooden plate inserted in the bottom. Strong similarities to Harold Burke's work.

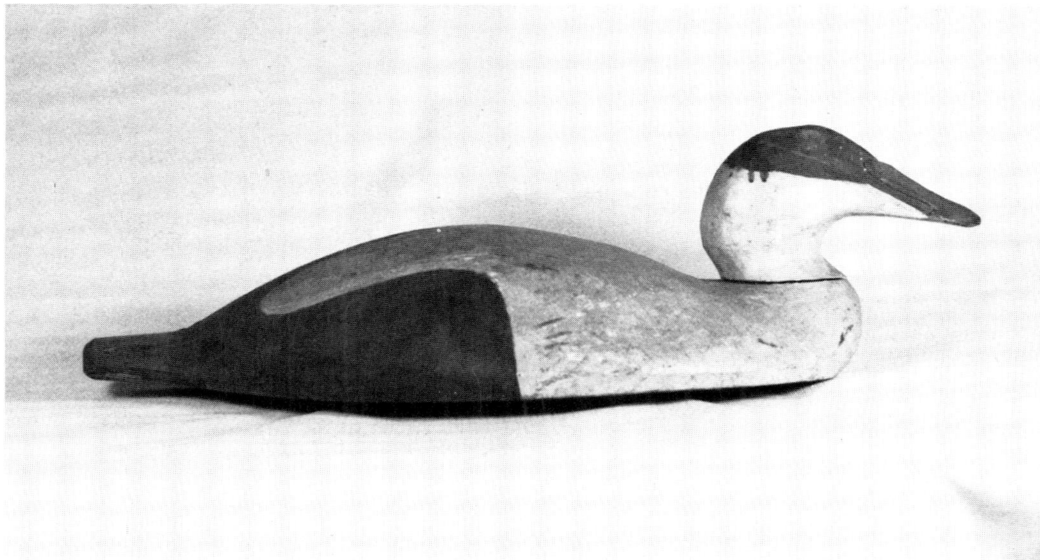

Eider drake from Drumhead, Nova Scotia, circa 1930.

Preening merganser hen by Gerald Matt, Little Dover, Nova Scotia, circa 1945.

Teal from the eastern shore of Nova Scotia, circa 1925. This small decoy is interesting in that the entire head is made of leather.

Eider hens and drakes made by Wellington Rafuse, Forchu Bay, Nova Scotia, circa 1940.

Merganser drake by Wellington Rafuse, Forchu Bay, Nova Scotia, circa 1930.

Blackduck by Erving Langille, Louisburg, Nova Scotia, circa 1950. Hollow and seamed through the center. The pattern for this decoy was taken from decoys which Langille purchased from a carver in Feltzen South, Nova Scotia.

Merganser drake from Seal Harbor, Nova Scotia, circa 1930. This decoy by an unknown maker is hollow with an inset wooden plate on the bottom. It was found with six hens by the same maker.

Plover found in Amherst, Nova Scotia, circa 1925. Probably used in the Tantamar Marshes.

Merganser hens and drake from Arichat, Cape Breton Island, Nova Scotia.

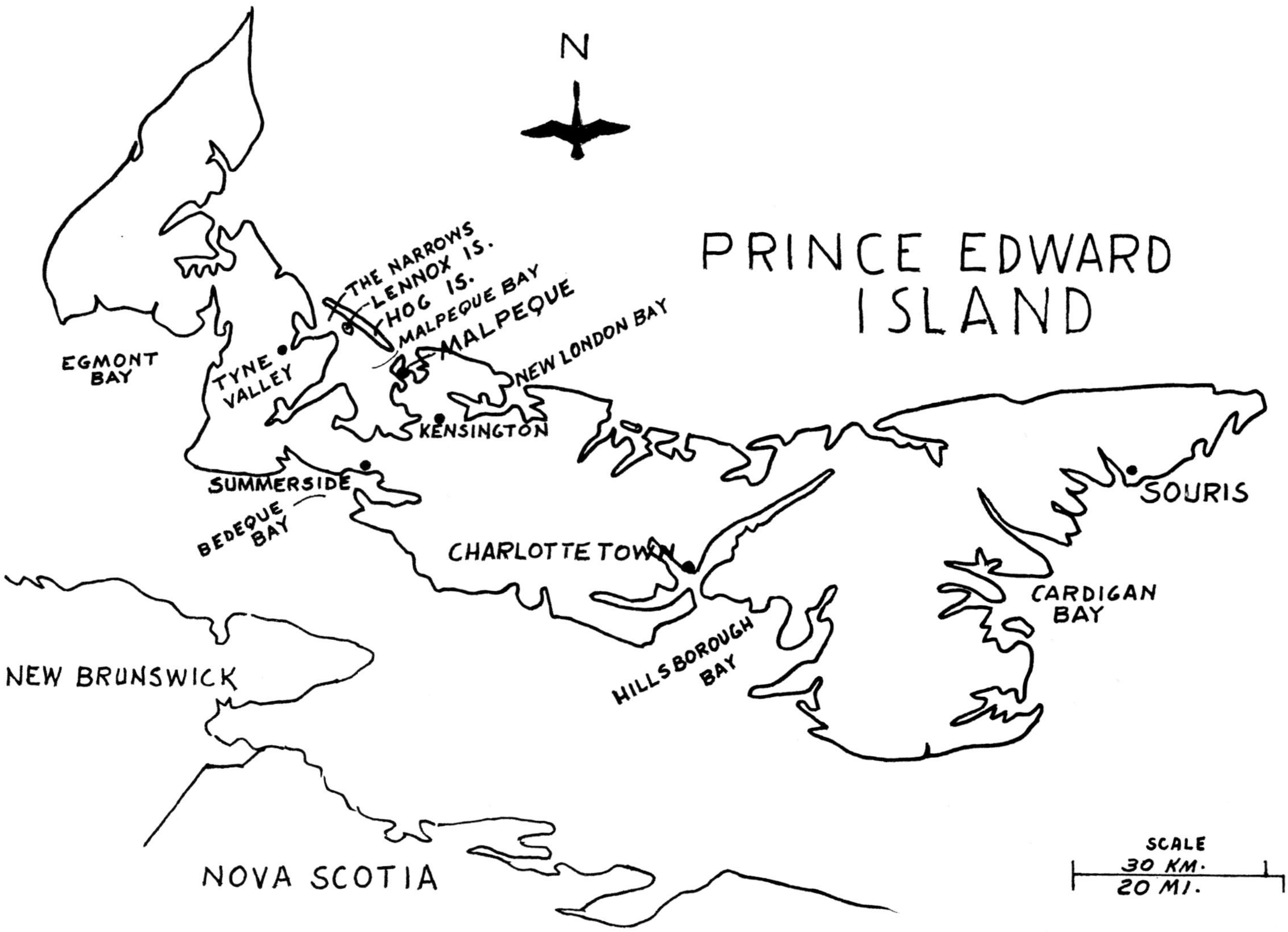

Part II
Prince Edward Island

Prince Edward Island is a crescent shaped island about 120 miles in length and varying from 3 to 35 miles in width. Its shores are heavily indented with deep inlets and large bays. Along the north shore where the water is warmed by an arm of the Gulf Stream, there is a long stretch of barrier sand hills. This barrier serves to protect several bays. It is shallow Malpeque Bay, the largest of the protected bays, along with New London Bay to the east and the Narrows to the west where one finds the highest concentrations of migrating birds. Here, in the spring and in the fall, great numbers of waterfowl rest and feed for two or three weeks at a time. Along the south shore where the water is much rougher and deeper, there is practically no bird hunting on the water, except in a protected northeastern section of Bedeque Bay and on the Hillsboro River.

The abundance of wildfowl on Prince Edward Island created an institution of market gunners and out of province sportsmen. In 1876, one visiting sportsman, John Rowan, recorded his impressions in a book. He noted that some snipe and blackduck breed on Prince Edward Island. In August golden plover, Hudsonian curlew, Eskimo curlew, sandpiper, and godwits leave their breeding grounds in

Golden plover in fall plumage by John Brooks, Freeland, Prince Edward Island, circa 1900. These split tailed plover decoys are from Brooks' own hunting rig.

The North Shore Hotel in Malpeque, Prince Edward Island, is now vacant and in a state of disrepair. However it was once a popular place of lodging for out-of-province sportsmen.

Brant by John Ramsay, Summerside, Prince Edward Island, circa 1890. Ramsay's carving style incorporated many of the natural positions of the live bird, a characteristic which is not uncommon among Prince Edward Island decoy carvers. →

Spring hunting using a sneak boat (with paddle wheels) and using goose decoys on the ice, is part of a bygone era of waterfowl hunting. (From an oil painting by Virginia Guyette)

Labrador and Newfoundland to spend about two months on the low sandy beaches and in the pasturelands of Prince Edward Island before continuing southward. Rowan also recorded four other kinds of plover, yellowlegs, sanderlings, and turnstones. It is not surprising then that shorebird hunting was considered exceptional. In 1810, the North Shore Hotel was built in the town of Malpeque and for many years it served as lodging for visiting hunters. They would travel by train to the Kensington Train Station and from there ride by horse and wagon or sleigh, the remaining twelve miles to the hotel. For shooting plover a hunter could hire a wagon to drive him along until he saw flocks of plover in a field. He would then put out his decoys and hide nearby while he waited to shoot. Sometimes, after a morning of shooting, families of the hunters staying at the hotel would picnic on plover roasted right on the spot. Extra killed birds were stored in the hotel ice house.

Perhaps the most dramatic wildfowl migration is that of the geese and brant. The geese generally begin to arrive in late March and stay for about one month before heading further north to their breeding grounds. In the fall they arrive in September and stay until mid-December before continuing southward. The brant arrive slightly later in the spring than the geese and stay for two months. In the fall on their southward flight they would land on Prince Edward Island in the middle of September, and leave a week or two before the geese in December. Prior to about 1930 the geese were hunted primarily on the coastal water or during the times when they came inland for fresh water. Brant and geese are similar in most of their habits and for both, the eel grass which they found out on the mud flats or along the shore, was their primary food source. The brant, however, have a strong dislike of land and seldom leave the salt water. They prefer to stay on the shallow bays and along the muddy shores. In the late 1920's the eel grass began to die off and the geese began increasingly to come in off the water to feed in the cornfields. The brant thrugh found it more difficult to adapt and eventually all but disappeared from the area. Those that exist there today must feed on small shellfish and invertabrates. It is interesting to note that, although the brant was once considered the finest tasing of the waterfowl, today it reportedly tastes terrible and fishy, a result one must assume of the change in diet.

As the habits of the geese changed so did the types of decoys used to lure them. In particular the field goose decoy was developed for use in the cornfields where the geese now regularly feed. A field decoy is simply a full bodied, round bottomed goose, mounted usually on three metal spikes, though they may also be wooden. Goose decoys had been used in the fields occasionally before but generally they were decoys designed for other types of hunting. Ice hunting in the spring needed a special decoy design. One type of ice goose decoy used, was the stick decoy, (in some areas referred to as an Indian decoy). This was a stick carved to resemble the head and neck of a goose. It was stuck into a mound of ice and mud which served as a body. At other times a pile of seaweed might be used for a body. Another type of ice goose decoy was the full bodied, round bottomed decoy with two wooden legs mounted on a wooden plank which held it upright and did not melt into the ice as metal spikes could. This was simply placed on the ice where needed. In the fall, flat bottomed floating goose decoys were used on the shallow water of the bays. Brant, blackduck and goose decoys were sometimes mounted on a single two or three foot long stake for use on the mud flats, and sometimes along the shore. The brant in particular liked to rest on the mud flats as the tide ebbed. A hunter would have to find or construct a sand bar on which he would arrange his decoys. When the moment was right he would shoot from his camouflaged punt boat. Flat, two dimensional, but fully painted silhouette or profile decoys were also used on the flats and later, more commonly in the field. Until it was made illegal in 1935 by international treaty, live geese and brant were sometimes used to lure in the wild birds.

The many shorebirds, blackducks, geese and brant, as well as various other species of duck made it possible for the market gunner to exist. One of the best known market gunners on Prince Edward Island was a man named Art Holland. He never carved a decoy in his life, but his rig of over 500 decoys consisted of the work of many different carvers. Most of Art Holland's decoys have been stolen, lost or sold and they are now dispersed over many parts of Canada and the United States. However, he did mark most of his decoys with his initials, so if you find one with "A. H." carved on the bottom you know it once came from his rig.

It is helpful when attempting to establish the age of these decoys to realize that field goose decoys tend to have been made later than about 1930, and not many people bothered to make brant decoys after this time because there were few brant to hunt. Shore bird decoys probably predate the final enactment of the Migratory Bird Act in 1928, which completely banned shorebird hunting. (Unfortunately for collectors, many shorebird decoys were taken from the shore and used as kindling or in some cases just plowed under in the fields where they had been set out.) It is likely that few ice decoys, used in spring hunting, were made after 1913, at which time spring hunting was made illegal.

As Prince Edward Island decoys go, it is the geese, the brant, and the shorebirds which stand out most dramatically. The style of shorebird carving to be found here is very similar to that which is found on Cape Cod and Nantucket Island. Because of this they are often mistaken as being of Massachusetts origin. Yet, it may be that the greatest expression of Prince Edward Island decoy carvers is in the sheer numbers and creative variety of goose and brant decoys. In addition, some good blackduck decoys, a few teal, and mergansers and a surprising number of fine seagull decoys may be found.

The story of wildfowl decoys on Prince Edward Island is an exciting part of North American decoy history and until now the information has been largely untapped. When one considers the abundance, quality and variety of decoys which have

Art Holland (1884-1979) was a very well known market gunner and later, a sport hunter, from St. Elenors, Prince Edward Island. For seventy years he hunted the waters of Malpeque Bay. He had several punt boats and a rig of over five hundred decoys carved by a dozen different Prince Edward Island carvers, as well as Mason blackducks and folding tin shorebirds made by Strater and Sohier in Boston. Art used just about every type of decoy available; Canada goose floaters and on ice platforms, brant floaters, brant on spikes, tin brant silhouettes, blackduck floaters, blackduck on spikes, teal, plover, curlew, yellowlegs of wood and tin. When possible, he carved a large A.H. on the bottom.

In 1968, at 84 years of age, Art was at his hunting camp on Hog Island, when a hurricane struck. As the water rose higher, he had to be lifted from the roof of his camp by a Canadian Services helicopter. Art was forced to leave his decoys which were washed away with the camp, but he wouldn't give up his shotgun.

come out of that one area, it is obvious that it is one of the more important decoy producing areas along the Atlantic Flyway.

For a long time, decoys have been hauled off Prince Edward Island. Malpeque Bay has yielded a treasure over the years. Though many local people carved decoys only for their own use, there were and still are quite a few commercial carvers who would sell decoys not only to other islanders, but also to the many out-of-province sportsmen.

One of the best of the early carvers was **John Ramsay** (1858-1934) of Summerside, Prince Edward Island. He worked most of his life at Hall Manufacturers, a Summerside based threshing mill producer. Although inspired to carve decoys after seeing those made by Havelock Mill, Ramsay clearly developed his own fine carving style. He did most of his carving in the early 1900's. He was a superb carver. His geese are hollow with a seam running from breast to just under the tail. The heads are applied to the neck and have tack eyes. He carved both ice geese and floater geese as well as brant, blackduck and shorebird decoys. The geese are painted with a deep burnt umber and feathered with greyish white brush strokes. John Ramsay was an artist among carvers. Most of his geese and brant decoys are carved in positions of action; breast and side preeners, attack positions, etc. He seems to have greatly influenced other carvers who also sought these action stances. As wonderful as many of the decoys by other Prince Edward Island carvers may be, none of them ever achieved the refinement and grace of form that is exhibited in the work of John Ramsay. The brant, when carved in normal upright position, use a two piece head and neck construction, while the breast preeners or attack positions generally have the head and neck all of one piece. Sometimes, if the wood was formed right, the entire brant (body, neck and head) may be carved out of one single piece of wood.

There was a great deal of travel back and forth between Prince Edward Island and parts of the United States so it is not surprising that John Ramsay's geese have turned up in the U.S. and been mistakenly attributed to an unknown American carver. (See page 181 of *Decoys of the Atlantic Flyway,* by Dr. George Ross Starr.) Over ninety of these decoys have turned up in the Malpeque Bay area alone. Most of them are from the rig of market gunner Art Holland, and others, marked with "J. B.", are from the rig of John Brooks, another Prince Edward Island carver and hunter.

John Brooks (1879-1962) from Freeland, Prince Edward Island, was a carpenter and sometime farmer and fisherman. He also worked as a guide for sportsmen, charging five dollars a day on hunting expeditions. He was a great outdoorsman and an ardent gunner. We are told that one moon-lit night, from inside his house, he heard the sound of geese approaching overhead. Grabbing his 10 gauge Ithaca shotgun and clad only in his underwear, he ran outside to get off a shot or two, and managed to quickly bring down fourteen of them.

Brooks would sink a tub in the ice to make a blind for spring shooting but more often he used a sneak boat. At first he used live geese for decoys but when this was outlawed he turned his hand to making wooden decoys. The bodies of the geese are hollow and seamed through the middle, and the head and neck are carved in one piece using tree branches. All of Brook's decoys clearly show the whittle marks but the geese show them more than the others. The effect is not one of crudity but instead is very appealing. All of Brook's goose decoys are painted a dark brown, the later ones being almost black, and have gray brush strokes for feathering. Brooks carved ice decoys and floaters in upright or feeding positions and all have carved eyes and mouths. His blackduck decoys are hollow with a seam through the body. They have glass eyes and there are floaters and stick-ups on iron spikes. He also carved brant which have tack eyes and are of both the stick-up and floater types. During the 1950's Brooks was given several carved winged teal decoys from Quebec from which he developed his feather carved teal decoys. When Brooks began to go gunning with Art Holland, Art showed him some goose decoys made by John Ramsay. Brooks made a rig of copies of Ramsay's decoys. They are extremely similar except for having slightly different paint and rough undersides. A further difference is that some whittle marks can be seen in Brooks' copies whereas on Ramsay's geese there are none at all. John Brooks sold some of his decoys to hunters. The ones in his own rig were all stamped with a "J. B.". However, twice in the past some of his goose decoys were stolen. Occasionally, one of these will surface today with the "J. B." gouged out and other initials carved in.

William Roy Mill (1901-   ) was born on Mill Point and later moved to Kensington. He is one of Prince Edward Island's best known commercial decoy carvers. He carved some brant and blackduck but by far the greatest number of his decoys have been geese. He began making decoys in 1934. His early goose decoy was quite stylish with a slender neck, delicately shaped head and thrust out breast. Many of the earlier geese had drop tails, this being formed by the addition of a piece of wood mortised into the body and shaped into a tail. As the demand for his decoys increased they became more simplified in form, the later ones having an easily identifiable large, even bulbous, beak. All of his decoys are made of white cedar, have a two piece head construction and tack eyes. When the demand for goose decoys for field use developed in the thirty's, Roy Mill is credited with being the first to use the now familiar three spike legs set up. The greatest number of his decoys are field geese and only a small percentage are floaters. Most of them are in an upright or feeding position and only a very, very few in any other position. Mill's decoys are carefully feather painted using his own secret paint mixtures, the formula of which he will not divulge though other carvers have tried to find out. He has, however, painted other peoples' decoys for them.

Another well known Prince Edward Island carver is **George Skerry** (1916-1965, from Lot 16, Prince Edward Island. Even though it has been many years since George Skerry made a goose decoy, they are still found scattered around the whole Malpeque Bay shore line. We've found them in fish shacks from Birchhill to Darnley and many are still in use.

George began carving and selling decoys in the early thirties. Although he was a carpenter, a boatbuilder, and a fisherman,

John Brooks, Freeland, Prince Edward Island, photo circa 1930.

he made and sold decoys part time all of his life. He carved several hundred geese, brant, blackduck, teal, plover and curlew; (shorebird hunting went on quite a while after it was outlawed in 1928). His decoys were always rootheads, were usually in elaborate positions, and all show the whittle marks very distinctly. His plover and curlew have carved wings. In general the quality of his carving varies tremendously, sometimes resulting in crude and clumsy but functional decoys and at other times resulting in decoys of remarkable grace and beauty.

Stacy Bryanton (1920-), Kensington, Prince Edward Island, is well known for his field goose decoys, sometimes described as cartoon-like. However, he also carved a few crows and gulls and some blackduck shadow decoys. He used the blackduck shadows in the early morning while waiting for the geese to come in.

Stacy bought five goose decoys from George Skerry to use as models and began carving his own rig. His first birds were fairly crude, still showing the whittle marks on the bodies and having screws for eyes. After some of his decoys were stolen, he marked his own rig by imbedding in the underside of the body a piece of metal with an "S. B." stamped on it.

As Stacy carved more and more birds to meet the ever growing demand for them, his geese became more elaborate with lots of feeders, sleepers, and his distinctive long necked sentinel goose. He also switched from screws to tack eyes and smoothed out the bodies. Most of his geese are also distinguished by a peculiar humped rise through the breast and shoulders to where the neck joins the body. Stacy's later goose decoys have a large "S. B." painted on the bottom and are supported on iron rods rather than three spikes. He also eliminated the plywood center which he had previously used for strength in the neck and head. Stacy's later work included many of the more elaborate positioned birds, including attackers, breast preeners, open bills, etc. He also made three oversized flying geese with glass eyes which were never used to decoy.

Stacy's silhouette geese usually had an "S. B." stamped on the flat metal stake. In all he has made about 500 decoys.

Henry A. Leslie (1851-1916) was a general store owner and operator of the Brunswick House hotel in Kensington. He did a considerable amount of market gunning for the Boston market. His companions for this venture and, later on for sport hunting, were Jack and Doc Kier and also Erskine McNutt who was just a boy at the time. Most of their hunting was done off of Hog Island and Fish Island.

Leslie carved several hundred goose decoys in the early 1900's. They somewhat resemble John Ramsay's style of decoy but they tend to be thinner through the body, and the floaters have longer tails. Most of his ice goose decoys and seemingly all of his floating goose decoys are hollow with a seam running horizontally through the body and then up to just behind the neck.

Many of Henry Leslie's decoys are still being used by hunters on Malpeque Bay, but most of them have been repainted by Roy Mill or Stacy Bryanton.

Another of the many Eastern Shore, Malpeque Bay hunters and carvers was **Frank Ramsay** (1882-1966). A farmer from Beach Point, he hunted mostly with his brother, Everett, and also with Art Holland. His goose decoys have the typical Malpeque Bay two piece head construction and tack eyes. They were mounted on a long single iron rod which was driven into the field or mud. Frank made one rig of approximately thirty geese around 1950 for his own use.

Kier Ramsay (1890-1981), a farmer, was born in Hamilton, Prince Edward Island, and was one of the big time hunters from the market gunning days. He used to hunt in the spring and fall with Frank and Billy Ramsay, and Billy and Kier Woodside. Their hunting grounds ranged from Hog Island on the north side of Malpeque Bay to Oyster Cove on the south side of Beach Point, and later on into the open fields on the back end of Kier's farm.

Kier carved around two hundred brant and goose decoys which were generally very plump. The brant may be distinguished by a raised and rounded shaping of the body where it joins the neck.

Roy Herman (1902-) was born in Pownal, Prince Edward Island, where he worked as an oyster picker and also operated a garage. He started carving goose decoys in the 1930's for his own use when hunting on Hillsborough Bay. He was one of the few decoy carvers on Prince Edward Island to use glass eyes.

Havelock Mill (1844-1900). Roy Mill's uncle was a farmer and fisherman who lived on Mills Point on the eastern side of Malpeque Bay. His favorite hunting area was near Hog Island, a very low island which was good for blinds in the fall and for use as a base in the spring.

Havelock carved blackduck, brant, geese and plover. His many brant floaters have a two piece head construction and are what one could call a typical Prince Edward Island brant decoy. The brant from his own rigs have rolled lead squares nailed to the bottom for weights. Unlike his brant floaters, his brant field decoys were made in a variety of preening and sleeping positions as well as the usual relaxed upright position. Most of Havelock's goose decoys were piled up and burned after a hunting accident which claimed the life of his son-in-law. The very few that have been found are wide and flat ice geese, made as sleepers with the head and neck lying flat on the center of the back. His golden plover have a split drop tail and his initials stamped on the bottom.

William MacLennan (1899-   ) from Tyne Valley, Prince Edward Island, carved approximately eighty geese and sixty or seventy brant decoys for his own use in the Inverness area and on Malpeque Bay. He also sold a few. His own rig has a "B" or "W" carved into the bottom of each decoy. Several distinct features are inset tack eyes, a rectangular weight set into the bottom and U-shaped feather painting on the backs.

Allen MacInnis (1885-1966) was an avid hunter and overall sportsman who worked as a sargeant on the Charlottetown police force during the 30's, 40's and 50's. He carved approximately 400 goose, brant and blackduck decoys for himself and for selling. He lived in Port Deroche and did most of his hunting there. MacInnis, who worked as a boat builder, built his own sailboat named "The Honest Cop".

Ralph Ramsay, 1982.

Ralph Ramsay (1890-   ) spent his entire life in the middle of the most active wildfowl hunting area in eastern Canada. When he was a young boy he retrieved (for a few cents) shot plover and curlew for the sportsmen staying at the North Shore Hotel in Malpeque. This was a convenient arrangement for him since one of the best shorebird hunting spots in Malpeque was the field across from his house. He began hunting in 1908 and even at 92 he still managed to get out for a few days of hunting. Although he made blackduck, plover and brant he is best known for his goose decoys and goose miniatures. Besides his own rig he carved 400 or 500 decoys to sell, most of which were field geese. One distinct characteristic is their squared off neck and head and the squared connection of the neck to the body. His paint is also distinctive and easy to identify.

Ralph's plover decoys met their end upon being discarded in a swamp in a footrace with a game warden.

Cyril Bulger (1937-   ), a fisherman from Foxley River, Prince Edward Island, carved a rig of goose decoys and several confidence gulls for his own use. The geese are large round floaters with good form and slightly glossy paint. The gulls have crossed wing tips, raised wings, and a bill carved out of the same piece of wood as the head instead of being applied.

Cyril, today, carves decorative mergansers, gulls and mallards.

Charlie Locke (1885-1966), a boat builder from Springbrook on New London Bay was one of the few Prince Edward Island decoy carvers to use the burning and scraping method for finishing off the bodies of his decoys. He carved around two hundred duck, goose and brant decoys, all of which were floaters. His geese have crossed tail feathers and the burned wood finish. They also tend to have extra long necks and are hollowed out underneath. One of Charlie's sons, Harry, many years later still used a large rig of these geese when hunting on New London Bay.

Eric Miller (1935-), an electrician from St. Elenors, Prince Edward Island, carved a rig of seven unique geese for his own use. They are all root heads with long snakey necks and heads carved from cedar roots. They have one hole drilled in the bottom for a single iron stake.

Adonijah Marks (1858-1945) was a highly skilled cabinetmaker and sleigh-maker from New London, Prince Edward Island. He carved several hundred geese, brant and blackducks for his own use and to sell. His geese and brant have raised wing outlines and crossed tail feathers. They tend to be large and plump, and are in many positions; preeners, attackers, sleepers, etc. Many of his brant have two thin iron rods coming out of the bottom as opposed to the usual one rod.

Paul Painter (1925-) and **George Jollimore**, both from French River, Prince Edward Island, together made a rig of twenty-eight feather carved geese with webbed metal feet. Stacy Bryanton later put heads on them and painted them. Paul Painter also made some goose silhouettes in various positions, including some with open mouths.

Ben Coughlin (1928-), a commercial fisherman from Freeland, Prince Edward Island, carved about two hundred fifty goose decoys to sell and for his own use when hunting on the north side of Malpeque Bay. He carved mostly floater geese with a small, metal, open box shaped stabilizer on the bottom, but he also carved a few field goose decoys. Coughlin also made some blackduck decoys, both floater and stick-up seagulls, and crow decoys.

Wendell Thompson (1939-), a farmer from Long River, Prince Edward Island, made approximately one hundred field goose decoys. Some were sold to various local hunters, and some of them he used in the grain fields near his home. Wendell's decoys are made with cedar body blocks and pine necks and heads. They have tack eyes and bent iron rods for legs. He still makes hunting decoys today which are a more realistic and refined version of his old ones.

Michael "Mick" Sark (Approx. 1875-1943), from the Lennox Island Indian Reserve, carved a large number of goose, brant, and shorebird decoys. In the spring and summer he would travel by boat along the north shore and Malpeque Bay, peddling and trading the decoys, oars, baskets and axe handles he had made the previous winter. His shorebirds with the bills pegged through to the back of the head, had simple yet pleasing lines. Michael's decoys were made of cedar, originally had no eyes and have an easily identifiable thick paint which shows the brush strokes. In the late 1920's and 30's, Michael and his family worked for Jim Tuplin and spent the winters in his summer home on the shore near Lot 11. During this time he made many brant and shorebird decoys for the Tuplin family, all of whom were avid waterfowl hunters.

Abram Thomas (1880-1965), from the Lennox Island Indian Reserve, was the most highly regarded decoy carver from that area. He didn't carve a great number of decoys but the ones he did make were known for their quality. Abram was a hunter and trapper who used to travel extensively by boat on Malpeque Bay and along the Conway Narrows. We believe that he is the carver of the excellent curlew and yellowlegs decoys pictured on page 78.

Eldred Simmons (1918-), a fisherman from Lot 16 on the south side of Malpeque Bay, Prince Edward Island, made over one hundred tack eyed plover decoys in the late 1930's. These shorebird decoys were probably used and sold well after shorebird hunting was made illegal in 1928, a practice that was common in the more remote areas of the maritime provinces. Eldred also made blackduck and goose decoys.

Marven Jackson (1937-   ), an electrician from Summerside, Prince Edward Island, carved a small number of goose decoys for his own use on Malpeque Bay.

Edwin MacFarlin (1889-1980) was a farmer from the town of Fernwood, Prince Edward Island. He also worked as a carpenter, blacksmith, and self-taught veterinarian. Edwin was an avid hunter and made a large rig of brant and goose decoys to use on Bedeque Bay and Salutation Cove, the latter of which bordered on his farm. His geese have long thin bodies and long graceful necks which make many of them very attractive.

Preening brant by John Ramsay, Summerside, Prince Edward Island, circa 1890. Ramsay's decoys are notable for their graceful lines and action poses. The body, head and neck of this brant are all carved out of one piece of wood.

Preening brant by John Ramsay, Summerside, Prince Edward Island, circa 1890. Body, head and neck are all carved out of one piece of wood.

Canada geese by John Ramsay, Summerside, Prince Edward Island, circa 1900. These goose decoys exemplify the two standard goose hunting methods in use on Prince Edward Island at the turn of the century. The one on the left was used on open water and the standing one on the right was set on the ice. Both are hollow and seamed through the middle. The head and neck of the ice decoy are made of one piece of wood.

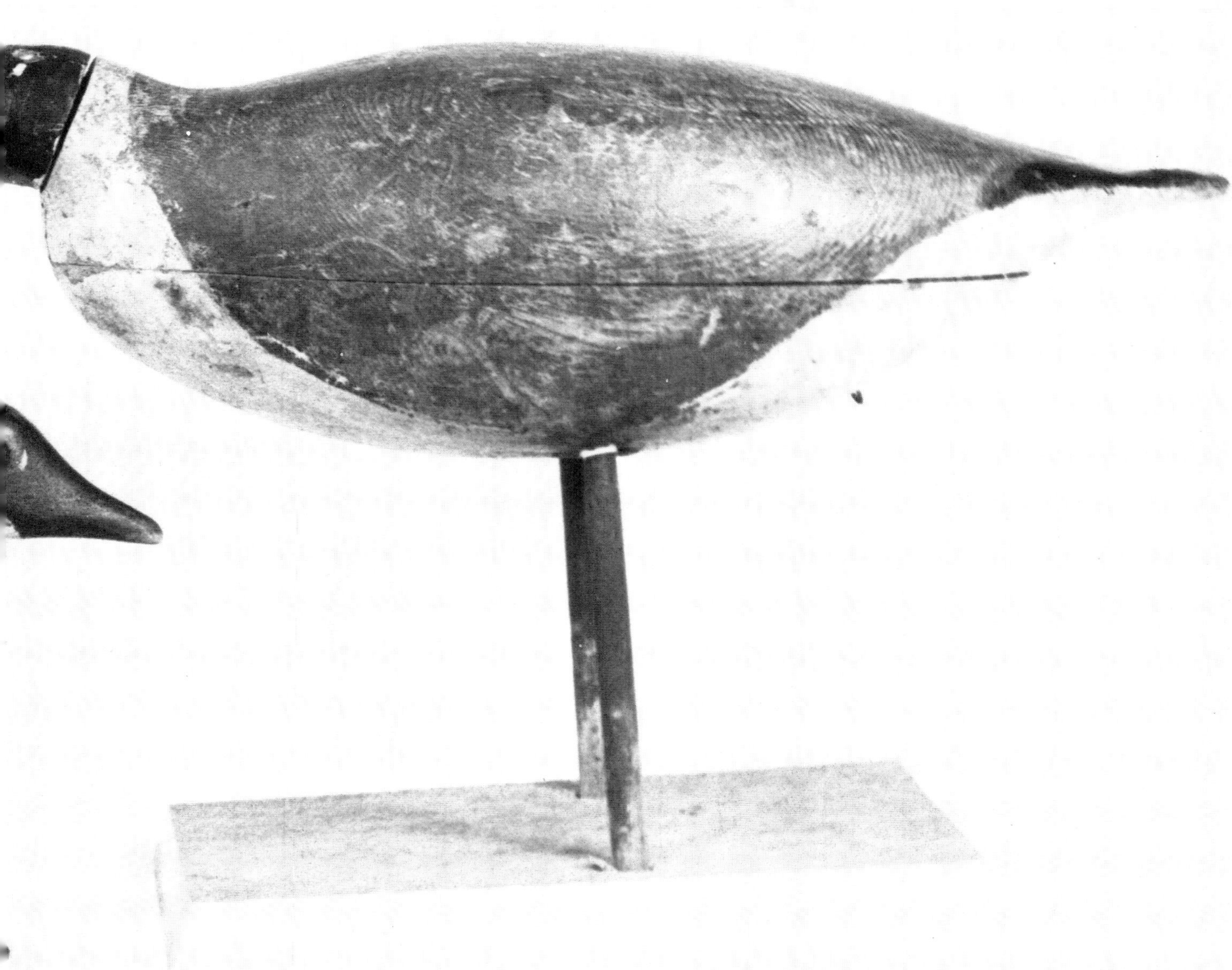

Black bellied plover, probably by John Ramsay, Summerside, Prince Edward Island, circa 1900. Sixty of these fine hollow decoys have turned up on Prince Edward Island at various times and from several different hunting rigs. With this form they might easily be confused with a shorebird decoy of Cape Cod origin.

Preening Canada goose by John Ramsay, Summerside, Prince Edward Island, circa 1900.

Golden plover (left) by John Brooks, Freeland, Prince Edward Island, and black bellied plover (right) by unknown maker, Malpeque Bay, both shorebirds circa 1900.

Canada goose on ice platform by John Brooks, Freeland, Prince Edward Island, circa 1935. Brooks' later goose decoys such as this one are smaller and have darker back paint than his earlier ones. The platform arrangement was convenient for use in field hunting also.

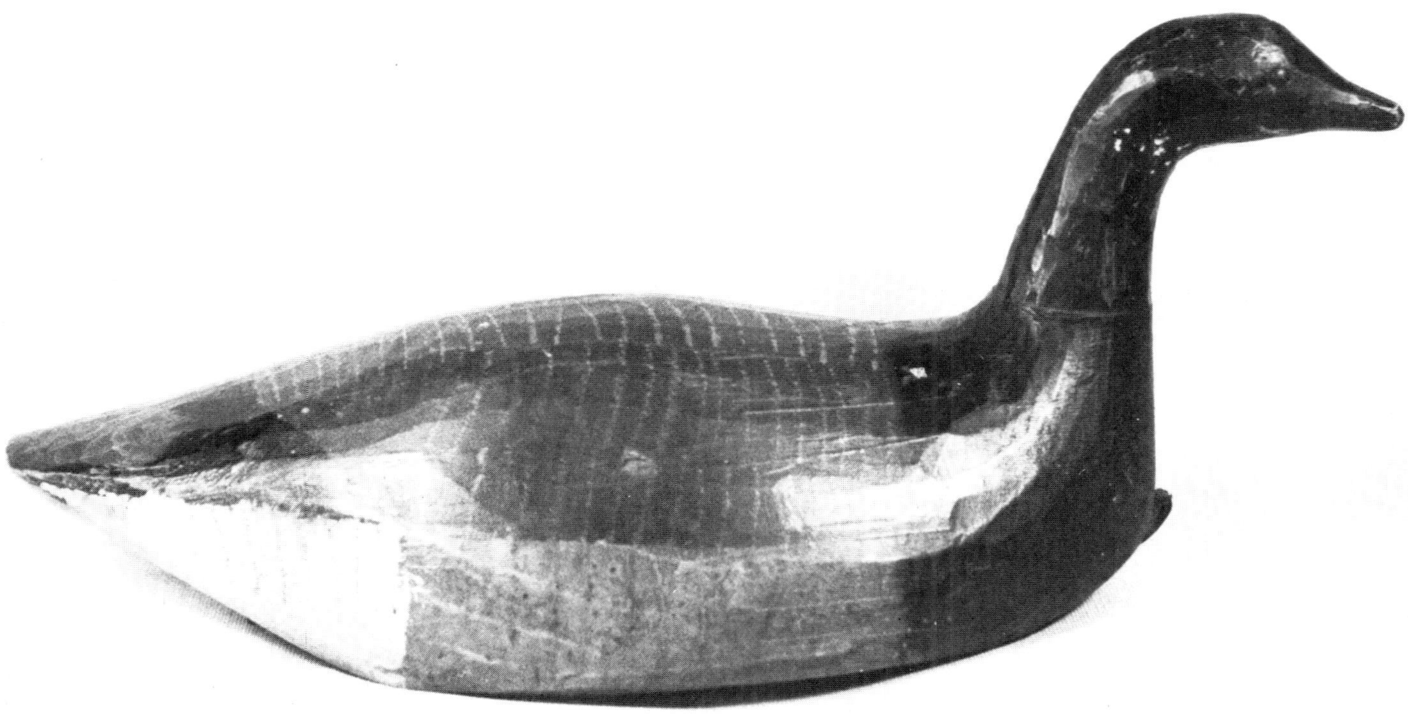

Brant by John Brooks, Freeland, Prince Edward Island, circa 1915.

Brant by John Brooks, Freeland, Prince Edward Island, circa 1920. This is a Brooks copy of a John Ramsay decoy. Though they are extremely similar the head shape is more Ramsay-like and it is slightly more refined then Brooks' usual work.

Brant on spikes by John Brooks, Freeland, Prince Edward Island, circa 1915. From his own hunting rig.

These Canada goose decoys are John Brooks' copies of goose decoys made by John Ramsay, circa 1920. The differences between Ramsay's work and Brooks' copies are: Brooks' copies show whittle marks, have a more squared off tail shape, the undersides show vertical saw marks, and the feather painting is a stronger gray.

Blackduck on spike by John Brooks, Freeland, Prince Edward Island, circa 1930. Hollow and seamed through the middle. From Art Holland's rig.

Blackduck on spike by John Brooks, Freeland, Prince Edward Island, circa 1955. Hollow and seamed through the middle. From his own rig.

Teal by John Brooks, Freeland, Prince Edward Island, circa 1955. Modeled after a Quebec teal decoy that he was given. From his own rig.

Canada goose decoys by W. Roy Mill, Kensington, Prince Edward Island, circa 1960. Late style field decoys.

Canada goose decoys by W. Roy Mill, Kensington, Prince Edward Island, circa 1950. Middle style field decoys.

Brant attributed to W. Roy Mill, Kensington, Prince Edward Island, circa 1935.

Canada goose decoy, by W. Roy Mill, Kensington, Prince Edward Island, circa 1935. Early dropped tail style field decoy.

Canada goose floater decoys by W. Roy Mill, Kensington, Prince Edward Island, circa 1935 (top) and 1955 (bottom).

Miniature Canada geese by W. Roy Mill, Kensington, Prince Edward Island, circa 1965.

Feeding Canada goose by George Skerry, Lot 16, Prince Edward Island, circa 1940. All of Skerry's duck and goose decoys were of roothead construction. This one is mounted on three metal rods for field use.

Canada goose with lifted wing by George Skerry, Lot 16, Prince Edward Island, circa 1940. Many of Skerry's goose decoys were mounted on a single iron rod for field use.

Curlews by George Skerry, Lot 16, Prince Edward Island, circa 1938.

Canada goose decoys by Stacy Bryanton, Kensington, Prince Edward Island, circa 1955. His earlier style field decoys.

Canada goose decoys by Stacy Bryanton, Kensington, Prince Edward Island. These field decoys are of various ages but are typical of his later style.

Late flying Canada goose by Stacy Bryanton, Kensington, Prince Edward Island.

Canada goose silhouette by Stacey Bryanton, Kensington, Prince Edward Island, circa 1960. This decoy has an "S.B." stamped into the flat iron stake, signifying that it was from his own hunting rig.

Hollow Canada goose in sleeping position, found in Kensington, Prince Edward Island, circa 1900. This decoy is very similar in style to decoys made by John Ramsay and Henry Leslie, but it was probably made by another Malpeque Bay area carver.

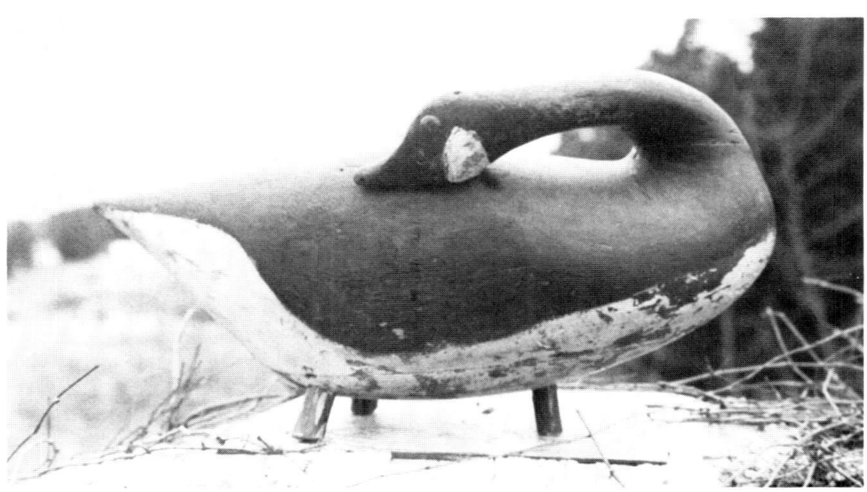

These metal footed field decoys are the combined work of Stacy Bryanton and Paul Painter, both of Prince Edward Island.

Hollow Canada goose by Henry Leslie, Kensington, Prince Edward Island. Henry made hundreds of goose decoys in the late 1800's and early 1900's for his own use as a market gunner.

Hollow Canada goose by Henry Leslie, Kensington, Prince Edward Island, circa 1880.

One of fourteen merganser decoys which were found in Northern, Prince Edward Island, and were probably made there around 1930. Very few merganser decoys were made and used on Prince Edward Island at all.

Stick up brant from Hamilton, Prince Edward Island, circa 1910.

Canada goose decoys on wooden stakes by Frank Ramsay, Hamilton, Prince Edward Island, circa 1950.

Canada goose decoy attributed to Harold Bierstow, Charlottown, Prince Edward Island.

Sleeping brant by Kier Ramsay, Hamilton, Prince Edward Island, circa 1910.

Canada goose field decoys by Kier Ramsay, Hamilton, Prince Edward Island, circa 1910.

Goose by Roy Herman, Pownal, Prince Edward Island, circa 1930. From his own hunting rig.

Sleeping goose by Havelock Mill, Mill's Point, Prince Edward Island, circa 1880. This decoy was originally mounted on an ice platform.

Preening goose by Roy Herman, Pownal, Prince Edward Island, circa 1920. Herman was one of the few Prince Edward Island carvers to use glass eyes in his decoys.

Brant floater decoy by Havelock Mill, circa 1880. From his own hunting rig.

Canada goose with root head construction by Havelock Mill, Mill's Point, Prince Edward Island.

Brant on iron rod by Havelock Mill, Mill's Point, Prince Edward Island, circa 1870.

Preening brant by Havelock Mill, circa 1880.

Seagull on two wooden stakes from Freeland, Prince Edward Island.

Brant by William MacLennan, Tyne Valley, Prince Edward Island, circa 1925. The preener's bill is mortised into it's back.

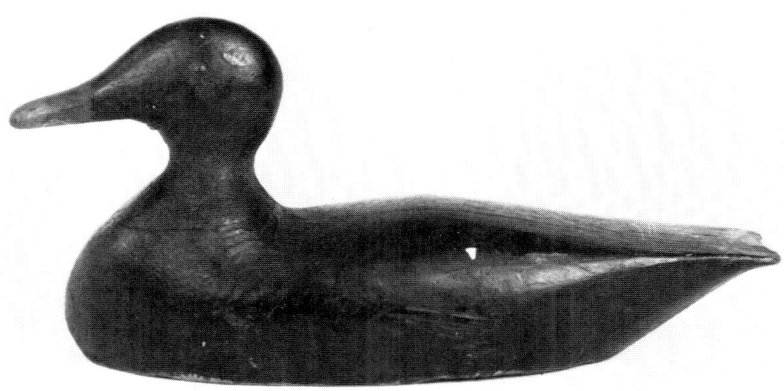

Blackduck by William MacLennan, Tyne Valley, Prince Edward Island. All of MacLennan's decoys have a rectangular lead weight set into the bottom.

Goose on ice platform by Allen MacInnis, Port DeRoche, Prince Edward Island, circa 1920.

Oversize yellowlegs, 14½" long, from Malpeque Bay, Prince Edward Island, circa 1900.

Canada goose with roothead construction found near Summerside, Prince Edward Island.

Brant silhouette from Malpeque Bay, Prince Edward Island, circa 1890.

Canada goose field decoys by Ralph Ramsay, Malpeque, Prince Edward Island, circa 1945.

Feeding goose by Eric Miller, St. Elenor's, Prince Edward Island. The head and neck are made from a cedar root.

Two yellowlegs from Art Holland's rig, circa 1910. A full time hunter, Art Holland had over five hundred decoys made by a dozen different carvers, as well as Mason blackducks, and folding tin shorebirds from the Strater and Sohier decoy factory in Boston.

One of seven goose decoys with root head construction, carved by Eric Miller of St. Elenors, Prince Edward Island. One of the other six had a raised wing which was formed by the natural shape of the wood. The one pictured here has an applied raised wing.

Hollow goose by Charlie Locke, Springbrook, Prince Edward Island, circa 1925. This is one of the few examples on Prince Edward Island of the burn and scrape method of finishing decoys.

Oversized Canada goose by Cyril Bulgar.

Several groups of these plump, tack eye yellowlegs have turned up in various places along the eastern shore of Malpeque Bay. Many Cape Cod shore bird decoys also show these typical Prince Edward Island characteristics. We feel that quite a few of the Prince Edward Island shorebird decoys that have been brought on the market over the years have been mislabeled because of these similarities.

Gull by Cyril Bulgar, Foxley River, Prince Edward Island.

Gull by Cyril Bulgar, Foxley River, Prince Edward Island. This is one of Cyril's first attempts at carving.

Attacking brant by Adonijah Marks, Margate, Prince Edward Island, circa 1910.

Canada goose silhouettes by Paul Painter, French River, Prince Edward Island.

Swimming goose by Ben Coughlin, Freeland, Prince Edward Island.

Canada goose field decoy by Wendell Thompson, Long River, Prince Edward Island.

Brant on spikes by Michael Sark, Lennox Island Indian Reserve, Prince Edward Island, circa 1930. From the Tuplin rig.

Golden plover by Michael Sark, Lennox Island Indian Reserve, Prince Edward Island, circa 1925. From the Tuplin rig.

Plover decoy by Eldred Simmons, Lot 16, Prince Edward Island, circa 1938.

Blackduck by Eldred Simmons, Lot 16, Prince Edward Island, circa 1940.

Canada goose by Marven Jackson, Summerside, Prince Edward Island, circa 1960.

Hollow Canada goose on an ice platform, circa 1920. Dozens of these stylish decoys have turned up on Prince Edward Island and in Nova Scotia, but so far their maker remains anonymous.

Black bellied plover (right), and golden plover (left), by unknown carvers from the eastern shore of Malpeque Bay, Prince Edward Island.

Tin brant silhouettes from Malpeque Bay, Prince Edward Island, circa 1900.

Hollow geese from Montegue, Prince Edward Island, circa 1880. Most of the goose decoys from this rig were burned in the 1970's when they became infested with hornets.

Canada goose by Edwin MacFarlin, Fernwood, Prince Edward Island, circa 1920.

Premier grade Mason goose, Detroit, Michigan, circa 1900. Quite a few Prince Edward Island hunters used goose, teal, blackduck, and yellowlegs decoys made by the Mason Decoy Factory.

Canada goose decoy on spikes from Bedeque Bay, Prince Edward Island, circa 1920.

Merganser hen from Hamilton, Prince Edward Island, circa 1910. This merganser was found with one by Keyes Chadwick and is assumed to be a local copy.

Brant by unknown maker from New London Bay, circa 1890. Many carvers from the New London area made their goose and brant decoys with crossed wing tips, a regional trait that was probably started by Adonijah Marks.

Alert tin brant silhouette from Malpeque Bay, Prince Edward Island, circa 1900.

Brant on spike from Malpeque Bay, Prince Edward Island, circa 1900.

Canada goose field decoys from Tyne Valley, Prince Edward Island, circa 1940.

Canada goose decoy on ice platform from Summerside, Prince Edward Island.

Golden Plover from Souris, Prince Edward Island, circa 1890. Hollow, tack eye shorebirds like this one were once common in the Souris area.

Canada goose decoys from Hillsborough Bay, Prince Edward Island.

Brant by an unknown carver, Malpeque Bay, Prince Edward Island, circa 1900.

Canada goose cane or stick decoy from the Alberton area, Prince Edward Island.

Brant from Rustico, Prince Edward Island, circa 1910.

Canada goose on wooden ice platform, from New London Bay, Prince Edward Island, circa 1910.

Brant on wooden stake, Malpeque Bay, Prince Edward Island, circa 1900.

Hollow geese from Wellington, Prince Edward Island, circa 1900.

Blackducks in various positions, Malpeque Bay, Prince Edward Island.

N
QUEBEC
CHALEUR BAY
MISCOU ISLAND
CARAQUET
ATLANTIC
OCEAN
TRACADIE
NEW
BRUNSWICK
TABUSINTAC RIVER
TABUSINTAC BAY
NEGUAC
MIRAMICHI BAY
MIRAMICHI RIVER
PRINCE EDWARD ISLAND
SALMON RIVER
CAPE TORMENTINE
BAIE VERTE
GRAND LAKE
TANTAMAR MARSHES
ST. JOHN RIVER
FREDERICTON
GAGETOWN
NOVA
MAINE
SAINT JOHN
SCOTIA
BAY OF FUNDY
GRAND MANAN ISLAND
SCALE
30 KM.
20 MI.

Part III

New Brunswick

In the early 1700's when the French Acadians first arrived in New Brunswick, they found an abundance of waterfowl to hunt along the coast. In the unsettled interior, all along the St. John River with its many islands, marshes and swamps, there was also excellent duck shooting to be had. The stretch of the Salmon River to Grand Lake and the bays and tributaries leading southward to the Bay of Fundy were the preferred haunts of many species of waterfowl, especially blackduck, whistler, bufflehead and bluebill. The best snipe hunting was reportedly found on the Tantamar Marshes, to the east of the Bay of Fundy, and indeed this is where a few New Brunswick shorebird decoys have turned up. But the evidence in decoys doesn't lead one to believe that many New Brunswick hunters bothered going after shorebirds for it is fairly unusual for a shorebird decoy to turn up in New Brunswick at all.

The eastern shore of New Brunswick from Baie de Chaleurs, near the Quebec border, to Baie Verte has long been appreciated by local sportsmen for the fine hunting of geese, brant and blackduck. Gunners could also go after old squaw, merganser and the now extinct Labrador duck. Early accounts of the area describe immense flocks of eider and several varieties of scoter but few decoys of these birds are found here today. Of foremost importance is the part of that coastline which extends northeast from the Miramici Bay, including Miscou Island, and the coastline through to Caraquet. There, a small shallow bay just north of the Miramici called the Tabusintac, has attracted enthusiastic hunters from all over eastern North America. They come to this bay because every fall many thousands of Canada geese, and formerly the brant, stop here to rest and feed among the eel grass flats, sandbars and low islands. Brant geese were once as numerous as the Canada goose in this area but during the 1930's, when the eel grass died off, the brant stopped coming. The eel grass has come back and the brant population has increased but the brant still usually avoid most of eastern Canada, including Tabusintab Bay. The harvesting of geese, brant and blackduck was made on a grand scale along this eastern New Brunswick shore and when we look at the decoys used here it is almost entirely these three birds which we find.

The wooden decoy as we know it today was in use in New Brunswick at least as early as 1800. There is furthermore much evidence to suggest that when the white man first arrived in New Brunswick in the 1600's, the Mic Mac Indians there were already using a particular type of decoy to hunt geese. In the early spring a hunter (in the Mic Mac method) would assemble about sixty or so bundles of seaweed on a field of ice near open water and would put a block of ice in front of each pile to simulate the white breast of the goose. A stick would be added to each of about a dozen piles to represent the head and neck. It is this seaweed decoy which some of the older hunters and guides call "Indian decoys". This type of decoy has been used by some hunters to lure geese until even a few years ago. Where the stick has survived the hunt and the years it is often referred to as a stick-goose decoy. It is generally painted black with white paint applied for the gills. However, early accounts of using this type of decoy in New Brunswick call for the preparation of the stick by charring and the white gills made by whittling to lighter wood. This charring and scraping method used by the Mic Mac Indians, gained wide usage in New Brunswick as a finishing method for wooden decoys in general. Many New Brunswick decoys are not painted except for the black neck and white markings of the geese and brant. The blackduck decoys often have no paint at all. Instead they show a darkening of the wood grain from being charred and scraped. In some cases the whole decoy is finished by oiling. This method is used by decoy makers today as it has been for many years past. The old ones however take on a certain velvety appearance from wear and acquired patina.

Spring hunting, now illegal, generally involved using flat bottomed floating decoys or full bodied decoys on legs with platforms. The full bodied floaters could be anchored in the water but the platform type was set out on the ice near the open water of the feeding grounds of the geese. Punt boats or paddle boats, camouflaged with chunks of ice if possible, carried the hunter within easy shooting range.

In the fall a person could hunt on the inland waterways by canoe. This was often accomplished at night, a practice which is now illegal. The Westmoreland County coast is one of the very few areas in New Brunswick where geese were hunted in the grain fields. Stick-up silouette or full bodied decoys would be used. Also commonly used in this area is a sort of sandbox hunting method of digging a hole in the sand, piling driftwood around it and laying out decoys. This method is reportedly also a Mic Mac Indian method originally used to hunt seagulls. The seagulls would be lured by bait mixed with seaweed spread around the driftwood. As they landed to grab the bait, a hunter waiting in the hole could reach up and grab a bird by the legs, apparently without scaring off the remaining birds .

In the Tabusintac area a popular method of fall hunting is with the use of the sink box. Briefly, this involves using an oblong box, long enough to lie down in and weighted down with rocks or lead to the level of the water. It would be steadied by wooden or canvas flaps on hinges and the whole thing was usually painted a dull grey. Thirty to eighty wooden floating geese, brant and blackduck decoys would be set out around the box. It could only be used when the tide was in. The sandbox also used in the Tabusintac area, is similar to the sink box except that it is designed to be buried in the sand or mud instead of floating in open water. In nearby Tracadie Bay a type of anchored, non-floating sink box is used. Above the water it appears to be the same coffin-shaped box with wing boards, but below the water it is mounted on legs buried in the mud. The entire box can be raised or lowered with the tide by turning four screw-like mechanisms on the legs.

The iron decoy probably appeared in New Brunswick around the turn of the century. They were used almost exclusively on Tabusintac Bay as ballast on the wings of sink boxes, the number used varying from two to six. The water in Tabusintac

Sneak boat built by George Morrison, Tabusintac, New Brunswick, circa 1900.

On Tabusintac Bay using a sink box is still a legal and standard method of hunting. Because of the advantage this method gives a hunter, shooting is allowed only until 1 P.M.

Many of these small camps are scattered along the long, low, sandy islands that protect Tabusintac Bay. After setting up a hunter with sink box and decoys, the guide returns to one of these camps several miles away and waits until the hunter signals by standing up in his sink box that the guide's assistance is again required.

Bay was seldom more than chest high and in an effort not to lose the iron decoys they would be secured to the sink box with anchor rope. If a gunner got into trouble he simply pushed the iron decoys overboard and the anchor rope allowed the guide to retrieve them later. The sink box in the Tabusintac area was primarily used for shooting brant so the iron decoys found here are brant decoys.

New Brunswick had a market gunning era but it was local and would in no way compare to the eastern United States. The market remained local due to a lack of adequate transportation and long distances from major urban centers. (The entire New Brunswick population in 1900 was only 300,000 people).

Around the turn of the century, several gunning outfitters started businesses in the Tabusintac area which catered to sport hunters. These outfitters hired many local hunters as guides. One of the requirements a guide had to meet was to provide his own equipment including a boat and a full sink box rig of decoys. The typical spread of decoys usually consisted of forty geese, twenty-five brant, and fifteen blackducks.

Cormorant or Shag shooting was carried on in New Brunswick on a fairly large scale. Although they could be hunted without decoys, New Brunswick seems to be one of the few places where cormorant decoys were used extensively. Fishermen felt that the cormorant badly depleted the fishing stock and considered them fair game. Local gunning outfitters encouraged their clients to come to their camps before the waterfowl season opened up to do some warm-up shooting in the "annual shag shoot". Thousands of birds were killed. They were not eaten but simply left where they fell. The government encouraged this carnage and as late as the 1940's was actually giving wardens and hunters free cases of shotgun shells to shoot cormorant. It is now realized that placing blame on the cormorant for depleting the fishing stock was greatly exaggerated but because of this belief the bird was not listed

The Tabusintac Camp, founded by Frank P. Loggie in 1900. Tabusintac, New Brunswick. For over fifty years this camp employed local guides and arranged brant, goose and duck hunting trips on Tabusintac Bay for out-of-province sportsmen.

in the 1918 Migratory Bird Treaty. Around 1965, complaints from the public and greater scientific knowledge about the cormorant finally legally ended the pre-season shag hunt. Many sportsman had ceased to participate before this date but the older fisherman still complain about the cormorant.

Herons were extensively hunted with decoys on Heron Island, located off the northern shore of New Brunswick towards the western end of Baie De Chaleurs, but few of the decoys can be found today.

A final interesting bit of information about New Brunswick decoys involves the use of seal decoys. Originally a Mic Mac device, it too was adopted and used by a few of the general population of hunters. The earlier ones were made from large pieces of driftwood but in later years they consisted of burlap stuffed with hay or seaweed. Successful deployment of seal decoys was dependant on the hunters ability to call like a seal. Very very few seal decoys have survived to this day.

New Brunswick's most interesting and well known carver is **Amateur "Mat" Savoie** (1896-), a self-taught barber, cobbler and folk artist from Neguac. Mat began carving working decoys when he was nine years old in 1905 and continued until the late 1960's. In addition to carving over five thousand working decoys and decorative birds, he made crooked knives, miniature animals, boats and sleighs.

The bulk of Mat's decoys are geese and blackducks made to sell to local hunters and to sportsmen hunting at the Tabusintac camps. He also carved a few bluebills, whistlers, brant and black-bellied gulls, and sold a lot of wooden heads to local carvers for use on their own decoy bodies. His first duck decoys were simple and show all the whittle marks. About 1940, he began smoothing out the finish on his decoys and using glass eyes. He also started deliniating the bills and setting in the nails connecting the neck to the body after which they were covered with a wooden peg. This stage of his work began the style most associated with him. Around 1955, Mat made "my secret tool", an iron stamp used to simulate body feathers which he used from this time on. Very few Savoie geese had the feather stamp markings however because it took too long to apply them and some hunters didn't like it. His last working decoys had very wide, two inch plus, heads. Much of Mat's later work is not only signed and dated but is also marked with the day's temperature in degrees Fahrenheit.

In the 1950's Mat began carving decorative decoys and bird carvings. He made flat bottomed style decorative decoys, a lot of half ducks that hung against the wall, and a very few full bodied standing ducks. He carved blackducks, geese, whistlers, pintail, bufflehead, mergansers, wood ducks, redheads, and seagulls. His prize decorative decoys are his preening blackducks, of which over four hundred were made.

John B. Wishart (1886-1968) and his father **John M. Wishart** (1843-1913) were the first fishing and gunning outfitters to go into business in the Tabusintac area. They set up their hunting camp on Wishart's Point around the turn of the century and it is still owned and operated by the Wishart family. The camp catered to American sportsmen who came there for goose, blackduck and brant shooting and salmon fishing. John M. and John B. carved thousands of goose and brant decoys for their own use as market gunners, and later on, for use in their camp. They also made blackduck decoys and cormorant silhouettes. The cormorant silhouettes were made from a one inch thick pine board.

Jim Gagnon (apx. 1890-1975) lived in Four Roads, New Brunswick, a small town just north of Tracadie. He worked as a carpenter and made decoys for himself and to sell to local hunters. He made at least several hundred goose decoys and a few brant. All were "rootheads", made from tree limbs or tree roots, and although primitive in appearance, were known to be

Amateur Savoie in his barber shop-workshop, holding a seagull that he carved in 1961, signed, dated, and temperature recorded (90° F.) Photo circa 1982.

the most effective decoys in the area. The goose decoys were finished with the char and scrape method. Because of Jim's use of tree limbs for heads, no two of his decoys are exactly alike.

Peter Ginnish (apx. 1880-1960) was a Mic Mac Indian from the Burnt Church Reserve near Neguac, New Brunswick. He guided for the Wisharts and other outfitters in the Tabusintac area and made several hundred goose and brant decoys to use in his work there. The bodies of his decoys were carved from cedar logs and were finished by burning and scraping. They were sometimes also coated with a mixture of boat tar and gasoline and then rolled in the sand to give them a rough textured appearance. The heads and necks were usually made from one piece of wood and were set on the body in positions of feeding, calling, upright, etc.

Jim Gatreau (1919-), from Lossier Settlement, a small town on the outskirts of Tracadie, New Brunswick. He began carving goose and blackduck decoys in the 1930's when he started working as a guide, since then he has made around two thousand decoys. Gautreau's decoys are made out of cedar, have a prominent broad tail, and usually but not always have raised wings. They are fairly narrow and some guides complain that they roll too much in the water. Gatreau's earlier decoys, vary more in form than his later ones. They also tend to be larger and rounder and the bodies were seldom painted but are finished by the char and scrape method. Hundreds of Gatreau's geese have been put on the antique market in the late 1970's and early 1980's, by Quebec pickers who bought them in northern New Brunswick, hauled them to Quebec and sold them into the market in New England where the newer ones are fairly common.

T. McAvity's Foundry in St. John, New Brunswick was opened in 1834. It designed, manufactured, and distributed many types of iron and brass products. They made marine equipment, railroad equipment, tools, fire hydrants, and "castings made to order". Around 1900, someone requested some iron brant decoys for use on the wings of the Tabusintac sinkboxes. They were made in the style of the typical New Brunswick brant decoy (unlike the flatter Chesapeake Bay style) and weighed forty pounds apiece. We know of approximately forty of these iron brant but assume that a couple of hundred were made. In the early 1920's McAvity's Foundry made another type of iron brant. It actually looked more like a large blackduck and had a handle built into the back. McAvity's Foundry closed for good in the 1960's.

Frank P. Loggie (1862-1939) was co-owner of the A&R Loggie Company which ran a number of canneries, lumber mills and general stores in New Brunswick, Nova Scotia, Quebec and Maine. In 1900 Frank bought a piece of property overlooking the Tabusintac River and built a hunting lodge there for himself and for entertaining Loggie Company guests. In 1918 Frank sold his lodge to a man from Florida who built it into the "Tabusintac Camp" which employed local guides and set up brant, goose and duck hunting trips on Tabusintac Bay for American sportsmen. Today the camp is owned by Bart Jacobs and operated by a local man named Ephrim Stymiest.

Frank Loggie's brant decoys (circa 1890) are what might be called the typical northeastern New Brunswick style decoy. They have simple bodies with raised tails and a slightly foreward leaning head and neck. They are probably the models used by McAvity's Foundry for their cast iron brant.

John Bailey (-1935) from Marysville, New Brunswick, a suburb of Fredricton, worked as a wheelwright for the MacFarlane Wagon company in nearby Nashwaaksis. Around 1900 he was talked into making decoys for several prominent Fredericton citizens who hunted brant and geese at the Tabusintac camps. Over approximately thirty years, John made between four and five hundred decoys. Because of John's precise yet fairly simple work, many people thought that his decoys were factory decoys. Over a hundred of these decoys are branded "W.T.C. F'ton" on the bottom and belonged to Bill Chestnut of the Chestnut Canoe Company. Others are branded "J.H. McM - F.N.B." for J. Harold McMurry. These two Fredericton men hunted in Tabusintac where they left many of these decoys. A number of copies of John Bailey's decoys have turned up in the Tabusintac area, some of which were made by Archibald Morrison.

Chief William "Bill" Polchis (aprox. 1855-1935) was a well known maker of Indian folk carvings on the Kingsclear Indian Reserve, north of Fredericton, New Brunswick. Around 1915, Fredericton businessman and sportsman, J. Harold McMurry, brought Bill a Mason paint eye blackduck to use as a pattern to make a hunting rig. Bill's copies of this decoy are a little cruder and narrower but greatly resemble the original. The weights on Polchis' decoys are printing plates from McMurry's printing shop in Fredericton.

Arthur Landry (1920-), a fisherman and then heavy equipment operator, from Inkerman, New Brunswick, made between one and two hundred decoys in the 1940's. He made mostly goose decoys but also made blackducks, whistlers, scoters and mergansers. They were all made of cedar and were usually finished by the burn and scrape method. The goose decoys were made in many different positions (sleepers, feeders, and watch ganders) with the head and neck formed from one piece of wood. Arthur also made several tip-up geese. (Imaginary head and breast submerged under water and tail sticking up in the air).

One of the many guides in the Tabusintac area was **Archibald Morrison** (1912-1980). Both he and his father, **George Morrison** (1866-1944), carved the typical Tabusintac Bay hunting rig of approximately forty geese, twenty-five brant, and fifteen blackducks, for use in working as guides for the Wisharts and the Tabusintac Camp. Archibald also made bluebill bodies on which he put Mat Savoie heads. His blackducks have tack eyes and all of his decoys were made of cedar. His brant decoys are less refined copies of John Bailey's decoys. Archibald's rig, with replacements and extras totaled about one hundred fifty decoys.

Amedee Doucette (1896-1975) was a guide who lived in the town of Fontaine, New Brunswick, until the late 1960's. At that time, the Canadian government disbanded the town when the National Park of Kouchibouguac was formed. He then moved to St. Louis De Kent. From 1920 to 1960, Amedee guided for the Smith family who were local gunning outfitters. They had a hunting lease on the Cardigan Plain near the mouth of the Kouchibouguac River. Amedee made geese, brant, oversized blackduck, whistler, and snipe decoys.

Carmen Johnson (1910-), a fisherman, hunter and trapper from Murray Corner in Cape Tormentine, New Brunswick, started carving decoys when he was fourteen years old. He made approximately seventy full bodied blackduck and goose decoys, and some scoter and goose silhouettes between 1924 and 1950, at which time he stopped carving. His blackducks are very small; about twelve inches in length, have a charred finish to give a dark brown color and have doweled on heads. Carmen's full bodied goose decoys were discarded and unfortunately destroyed in 1950 when he replaced them with a rig of silhouette geese.

Earnest L. Goodwin (1899-), a boatbuilder from Baie Verte, New Brunswick, on the Cape Tormentine penninsula, carved around two hundred whistler, bluebill, blackduck, and goose decoys. In his rig of fifty hollow goose decoys, many are designed as divers and are constructed with full bodies and necks extending to the water line but no head or neck below the water line. His blackducks are also hollow but the bluebills and whistlers are solid. All of his decoys were made of cedar and usually have his name stamped into the bottom. He also made half size decorative bird carvings.

Earnest L. Goodwin's father was New Brunswick market gunner, Earnest P. Goodwin (1865-1961).

Ralph Howlett (1890-) was the major commercial carver in southern New Brunswick. He was born in Newfoundland but moved to St. John, New Brunswick after World War I to work as a government agricultural inspector. He carved over two thousand working decoys between 1920 and 1960 which he sold for two, and later three dollars apiece. Ralph made both oversized decoys for use off the Fundy coast and normal sized decoys for use in the lower St. John River. He made mostly blackducks and whistler but also made some geese. His decoys are made of cedar, have glass eyes, and are in a forward leaning position. Most of his decoys show the rasp marks and have 2 inch to 2½ inch holes drilled in the bottoms.

A very well known St. John River carver and hunter was **Frank Duvernet** (1889-1964). He was a riverboat operator and sawmill worker from Gagetown, New Brunswick which is in the heart of blackduck country. Frank was a part time market hunter who would sell ducks locally for twentyfive cents each or ship them by riverboat to the St. John market. He produced between two and three hundred blackduck and whistler decoys and a few goose floater decoys. He also made some goose silhouette stick-ups. Most of the blackducks and some of his whistlers were oversized, weighing up to five pounds each. The oversize decoys had large square tails and the regular size decoys had V-shaped tails. Although Frank originally used painted nail heads for eyes, in 1945 he replaced them with glass eyes.

One of the few carvers known in the St. John, New Brunswick area is **Joseph L. Beckett** (1915-). He carved a small number of goose decoys and wood ducks. Beckett made his decoys mostly for use in the lower St. John River. The heads and necks of his goose decoys were made from the natural curve of a cedar branch and have ten 1½ inch holes drilled in the bottoms for buoyancy.

Henry Gilbert (1864-1948) was a sportsman from Rothesay, New Brunswick, who kept a house in Lower Gagetown to use as a base for duck hunting. He carved several hundred blackduck and whistler decoys and a few bufflehead. Henry's decoys were fairly basic but sufficient for hunting with the large concentrations of waterfowl in the Gagetown area. They had glass eyes and a half arch under the tail. Henry also was a sport fisherman who made fine fishing rods.

Lincoln Harvey (1921-), a Department of Fisheries officer from Woodward's Cove on Grand Manan Island, New Brunswick, began carving decoys in the 1940's. He made approximately thirty solid bodied whistlers with inletted heads and hollow blackduck decoys. In 1975 he began making decorative bird carvings.

Jim Zwicker (1849-1933) moved from Lunenburg, Nova Scotia to the town of Castalia on Grand Manan Island, New Brunswick, where, in the 1890's, he set up a business as a carpenter and commercial decoy carver. He made several hundred seaducks, whistlers, old squaw, and mergansers. His eider decoys with their graceful lines and pleasing paint patterns are among the finest made in Canada or the United States.

Joseph Green (1905-) worked as a fisherman in Seal Cove, Grand Manan Island for sixty-two years. He made around thirty merganser and whistler decoys to use while hunting on the ledges off Pond Point on Wood Island. His decoys usually had slightly raised crossed wings. Joseph used a punt boat which was painted brown to match the seaweed on the rocks where he hunted.

Allan L. Moses (1881-1953) was an internationally known naturalist and taxidermist from Grand Manan Island, New Brunswick. In his younger years he carved old squaw and seaduck decoys for his own use when hunting off of Grand Manan Island.

Moses was curator of the Cleveland Museum of Natural History from 1923 to 1926. In 1928 and '29, he worked at the American Museum of Natural History in New York City. While he was working there he accompanied J. Sterling Rockerfeller on a bird speciman expedition to Africa and found a rare bird. In 1930, as a reward for finding this bird, Rockerfeller bought Kent Island, near Grand Manan Island, for Moses to set up a bird sanctuary. The basic purpose of the sanctuary was for use as a breeding ground for the eider duck, which at the time was in danger of becoming extinct.

Mariner Wilcox (1845-1908) was a fisherman who lived on Wood Island, a small island in the Grand Manan Island group. He made several hundred seaduck and old squaw decoys to sell to local hunters. Around 1900, he sold sets of six old squaw (3 hens and 3 drakes) for five dollars a set.

Blackduck by Amateur Savoie, Neguac, New Brunswick, circa 1955. Feather stamped finish.

Brant by Amateur Savoie, Neguac, New Brunswick, circa 1940. The only known example of a brant decoy by Savoie.

Canada goose by Amateur Savoie, Neguac, New Brunswick, circa 1955. Unlike most of Savoie's goose decoys, this one has a feather stamped finish.

Sleeping blackduck by Amateur Savoie, Neguac, New Brunswick, circa 1960's.

Blackducks by Amateur Savoie, Neguac, New Brunswick, pre-1940 styling (lower), and 1940-1955 styling (upper).

Canada goose by Amateur Savoie, Neguac, New Brunswick, circa 1950.

Blackduck by Amateur Savoie, Neguac, New Brunswick, circa 1960's.

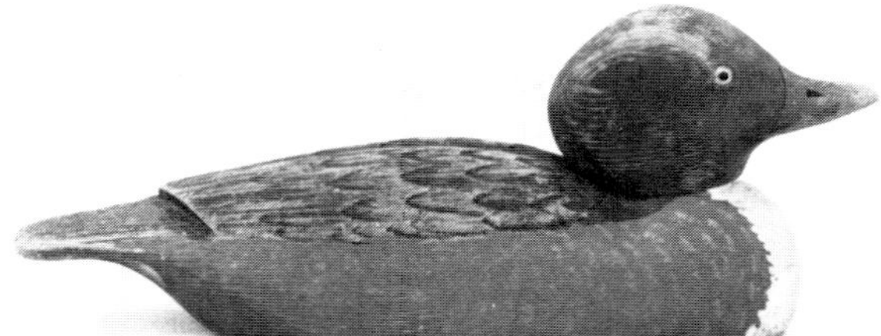

Whistler hen and drake by Amateur Savoie, Neguac, New Brunswick, circa 1955.

Whistler by Amateur Savoie, Neguac, New Brunswick, circa 1964. Savoie incorporated the most detailing in this last phase of his carving. This carving is signed, dated and marked with the days recorded temperature (15° F).

Canada goose by Jim Gagnon, Four Roads, New Brunswick, circa 1930.

Cormorant silhouette by John M. Wishart, Tabusintac, New Brunswick, circa 1925.

Brant by Peter Ginnish, Burnt Church Indian Reserve, New Brunswick, circa 1920.

Canada goose by Peter Ginnish, Burnt Church Indian Reserve, New Brunswick, circa 1920.

Canada goose in feeding position by Jim Gatreau, Lossier Settlement, New Brunswick, circa 1940.

Blackduck and Canada goose by Jim Gatreau, Lossier Settlement, New Brunswick, circa 1960.

Iron brant by T. McAvity's Foundry, St. John, New Brunswick, circa 1910.

Brant by Frank P. Loggie, Tabusintac, New Brunswick, circa 1890.

Iron brant by T. McAvity's Foundry, St. John, New Brunswick, circa 1930.

Canada goose by John Bailey, Marysville, New Brunswick, circa 1910. W.T.C. F'ton brand on the underside (William T. Chestnut's rig).

Brant by John Bailey, Marysville, New Brunswick, circa 1910. From the rig of Bill Chestnut and bearing his brand.

Hollow Canada goose from Tabusintac, New Brunswick, circa 1910. From the rig of Bill Chestnut and bearing his brand.

Blackduck by Chief William Polchis, Kingsclear Indian Reserve, New Brunswick, circa 1915. Polchis' copy of a Mason factory decoy.

Brant by Arthur Landry, Inkerman, New Brunswick, circa 1945.

Canada goose by Archibald Morrison, Tabusintac, New Brunswick, circa 1940.

Brant and blackduck by Archibald Morrison, Tabusintac, New Brunswick, circa 1940. Morrison's brant (lower) are copies of John Bailey's brant decoys.

Canada goose from St. Marys, New Brunswick, circa 1920.

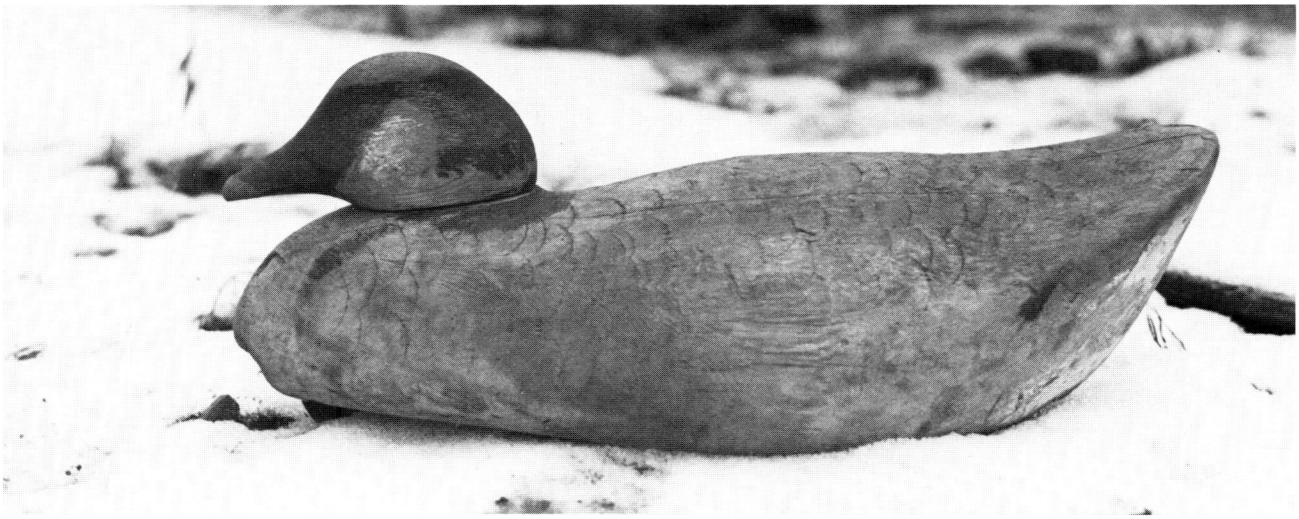

Canada goose in content position by Amédée Doucette, Fontaine, New Brunswick, circa 1930.

Blackduck by Carmen Johnson, Murray Corner, New Brunswick, circa 1935. Doweled on head and char and scrape type of finish.

Canada goose silhouettes by Carmen Johnson, Murray Corner, New Brunswick, circa 1950.

In 1939, F. Cedric Cooper, an active waterfowler from Fredricton, New Brunswick, gave thirty cedar blocks to a man he thought was named Willie Savoie and who was supposed to live on Tracadie Beach. This carver made Cedric thirty goose decoys which were branded F.C.C. on the bottom. Although several decoy collectors and historians have tried to verify the existance of Willie Savoie, none have been successful. So, for now, this decoy is listed as; Canada goose, circa 1939, Tracadie, New Brunswick.

Feeding Canada goose by E.L. Goodwin, Baie Verte, New Brunswick, circa 1930. Like all of Goodwin's goose decoys this one is hollow and is stamped on the bottom "E.L. Goodwin".

Canada goose by E.L. Goodwin, Baie Verte, New Brunswick, circa 1930. Hollow and stamped "E.L. Goodwin".

Canada goose by Ralph Howlett, St. John, New Brunswick, circa 1950.

Whistler drakes by Ralph Howlett, St. John, New Brunswick, circa 1950 (upper) and 1930 (lower).

Blackduck by Frank Duvernet, Gagetown, New Brunswick, circa 1920. Oversized.

Whistler hen and drake from Hampton, New Brunswick, circa 1930.

Blackduck from the lower St. John River area, New Brunswick, circa 1920.

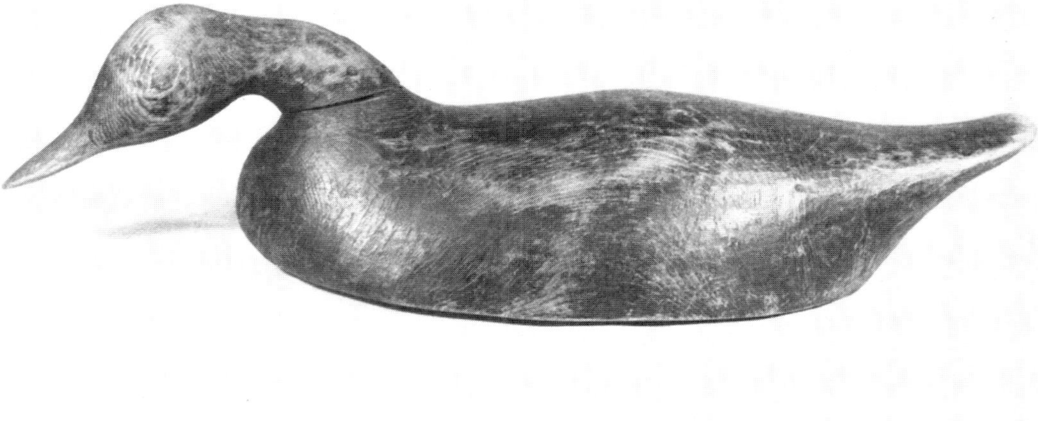

Feeding blackduck from the Tabusintac, New Brunswick area, circa 1920.

Sleeping Canada goose by Joseph Beckett, St. John, New Brunswick, circa 1950.

Whistler drake and blackduck by Henry Gilbert, Rothesay, New Brunswick, circa 1910.

Whistler drake from the Hamstead area of New Brunswick, circa 1935. Possibly the work of George Carol (1900-1974).

Bluebill hen and drake by H.W. Wilkins, Owen Sound, Ontario, circa 1955.

Blackduck by H.W. Wilkins (1875-1961), circa 1955. Wilkins was from Owen Sound, Ontario and although he sold a few decoys in Ontario, the vast majority (around 500) were marketed in New Brunswick.

Feeding Canada goose by Damien Rousseau, Tabusintac, New Brunswick, circa 1930.

Tip-up or diving goose with tree root legs, from the lower St. John River, New Brunswick.

Blackduck from the lower St. John River, New Brunswick.

Unfinished decoy of uncertain species but with interesting form, from Fredricton, New Brunswick, circa 1910. Notched tail.

Blackduck from the lower St. John River, New Brunswick, circa 1930. → ↓

Hollow Canada goose, Cape Tormentine, New Brunswick, circa 1910.

Whistler drakes from Grand Manan Island, New Brunswick, 1930. Styling characteristics are similar to Jim Zwicker's work.

Old squaw drake by Allan Moses, Grand Manan Island, New Brunswick, circa 1920.

Old squaw hen and drake by Mariner Wilcox, from Wood Island in the Grand Manan Island group, New Brunswick, circa 1900.

Auk silhouette found on the Bay of Fundy coast, length from tip of bill to tail, 14 inches.

Merganser drake and whistler drakes by Joseph Green, Seal Cove, Grand Manan Island, New Brunswick, circa 1940.

Blackduck by Lincoln Harvey, Woodward's Cove, Grand Manan Island, New Brunswick, circa 1945.

Blackduck and whistler drake by Lincoln Harvey, Woodward's Cove, Grand Manan Island, New Brunswick, circa 1945. The blackduck is hollow and the whistler has an inletted head.

Eider hen and drake, possibly from the Grand Manan Island group, New Brunswick. Maker and dates unknown. Signed C.F. Jacobs on the bottom.

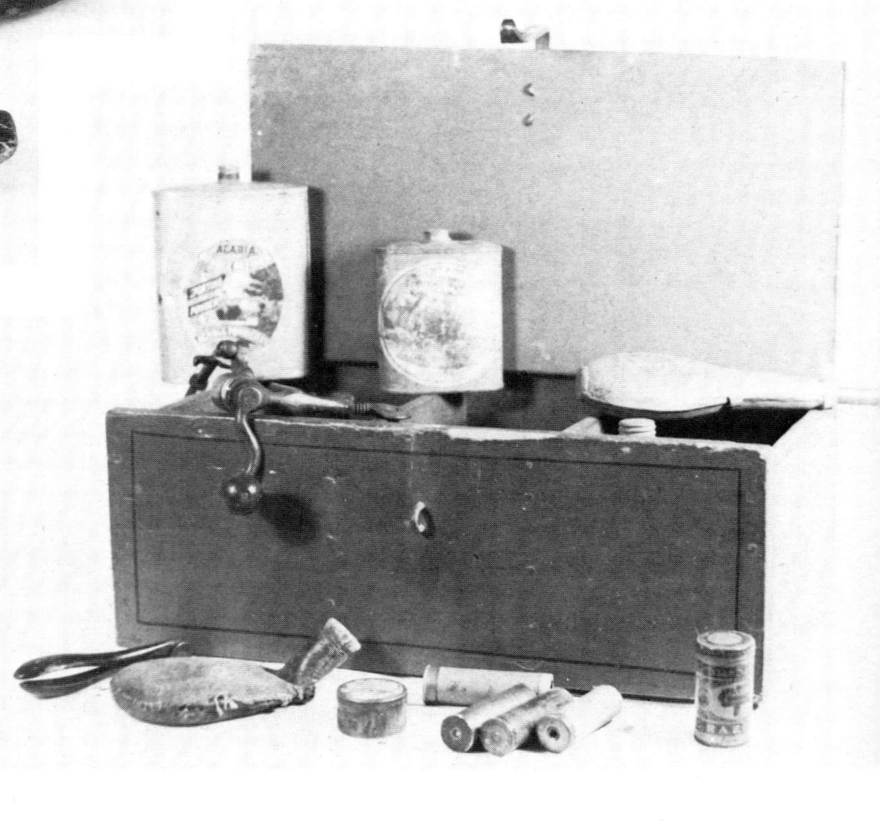

Gunning box with assorted gunning paraphernalia, St. Steven, New Brunswick.

THE END

SHOOTING DUCKS AT THE HALF-MOONS

October is here and it's time for some fun,
So fill up your knapsacks and clean up your guns,
Oil up your oilskins, hunt up your boots,
We're going to the Half-Moons to shoot at some coots.

There's Cliff Perry from Blanche, a gunner of old,
And Olson and Lloyd who knocks them stone cold;
There's Walter from Blanche who has a keen eye;
Ed Crowell from Port La Tour doesn't let many go by.

There's Emerson from Cape Negro, a gunner most bold,
He can knock down a few, so the story is told;
But gunners or liars, the six can't be beat;
In order to do that the winner must cheat.

With decoys all set, bad weather or fine,
They'll be looking for coots a-down the coast-line;
The birds come up and smother right in,
Then up go their guns and the shooting begins.

As they start to shoot they can see their wings fold.
So the story is told by the gunners so bold:
Oh, this is the way their story is told,
But what really happens, the truth I'll unfold.

The birds flutter about, but keep on the wing,
And I'm sure just a few felt a very slight sting,
The shooting was over, but not a duck fell;
But what can you expect a gunner to tell?

For it happens this way, many a time,
And O, the alibies that bunch sure can find!
"Why they run me right down, so what could I do?
I shot at the bunch but it must have gone through."

But they have lots of sport, of that I am sure,
And the way they go at it is sure no rest cure.
At four in the morning they are up with a bound,
And long before daylight they are out on the ground.

They work and they sweat, they puff and they blow,
They shoot down a cripple and Boy, how they row!
And they call it vacation, but's it's work I should say,
And half they do get are given away.

When the season is over it's "Gunning, good-bye",
"Don't feel a bit tired", but O, how they lie!
"Better luck, next year", they say and depart,
But they've greatly enjoyed the sport dear to their hearts.

-Written by the late George Smith, the late Capt. Mortimer Nickerson of Massachusetts and the late Capt. C.B. Kenney of Thomasville, Nova Scotia.

Hunters referred to in the poem are;
Clifford Perry, Orson Perry, Lloyd Perry, Emerson Thomas, Walter Myrick, and Ed Crowell.

Bibliography

Barber, Joel. *Wildfowl Decoys.* New York: Dover Publications, 1934.

Ingersoll, Keith. Unpublished works on Allan Moses. Fredricton, New Brunswick, 1982.

Mackey, William J., Jr. *American Bird Decoys.* Exton, Pennsylvania: Schiffer Publishing Ltd., 1982.

Monro, Alexander. *New Brunswick, with a Brief Outline of Nova Scotia and Prince Edward Island.* Halifax, Nova Scotia: Printed by Richard Nugent, 1855.

Porter, H.A. *Waterfowler's World.* "The Tabusintac Bay Sinkbox." Germantown, Tennessee: Waterfowl Publications, Incorporated, 1979.

Silver, Arthur P. *Farm-Cottage, Camp, and Canoe in Maritime Canada.* Toronto, Canada: Musson Book Company Ltd., 1907

Starr, George R., M.D. *Decoys of the Atlantic Flyway.* New York: Winchester Press, 1974.

Carver's Index

Backman, Edwin, Lunenburg, Nova Scotia (1872-1914)
Bailey, John, Marysville, New Brunswick (1865-1935
Baker, Robert F., Clam Harbor, Nova Scotia (1906-)
Beckett, Joseph L., Saint John, New Brunswick (1915-)
Bezanson, Guilford, Lunenburg, Nova Scotia (1893-1960)
Bierstow, Harold, Charlottetown, Prince Edward Island
Brooks, John, Freeland, Prince Edward Island (1879-1962)
Bryanton, Stacey, Kensington, Prince Edward Island (1920-)
Bulgar, Cyril, Foxley River, Prince Edward Island (1937-)
Burke, Harold, Drumhead, Nova Scotia (1888-1970)
Burt, Leslie, Spryback Bay, Nova Scotia

Carroll, George, Hampstead, New Brunswick (1900-1974)
Coughlin, Ben, Freeland, Prince Edward Island (1928-)
Cross, Harvey, Big Tancook Island, Nova Scotia (1895-1981)
Crowell, Oscar L., Smithville, Nova Scotia (1917-)

Doan, Al, Gunning Cove, Nova Scotia

Edwards, Clyde, Eastern Passage, Nova Scotia (1899-1976)
Ernst, Clarence, Indian Point, Nova Scotia (1912-)

Gagnon, Jim, Four Roads, New Brunswick (1890-1975)
Gardiner, Carroll, Dartmouth, Nova Scotia (1918-)
Gatreau, Jim, Lossier Settlement, New Brunswick (1919-)
Gilbert, Henry, Rothsay, New Brunswick (1864-1948)
Ginnish, Peter, Burnt Church, New Brunswick (1880-1960)
Goodwin, Earnest L., Baie Verte, New Brunswick (1899-)
Green, Joseph, Seal Cove, Grand Manan Island, New Brunswick (1905-)

Harvey, Lincoln, Woodward's Cove, Grand Manan Island, New Brunswick (1921-)
Hatt, Otis, Chester Basin, Nova Scotia (1871-1946)
Herman, Roy, Pownal, Prince Edward Island (1902-)
Hersey, Everett, Blanche, Nova Scotia (1898-1975)
Hiltz, Orran, Indian Point, Nova Scotia (1901-1978)
Hopkins, Bruce, Smithville, Nova Scotia (1949-)
Howlett, Ralph, Saint John, New Brunswick (1890-)

Jackson, Marven, Summerside, Prince Edward Island (1937-)
Johnson, Carmen, Murray Corner, New Brunswick (1910-)
Jollimore, George, French River, Prince Edward Island

Kaiser, Marshall, Sidney, Nova Scotia (1899-)

Lamerock, Frank, Reynoldscroft, Nova Scotia (1907-1977)
Landry, Arthur, Inkerman, New Brunswick (1920-)
Langille, Erving, Louisburg, Nova Scotia (1932-)
Leslie, Henry, Kensington, Prince Edward Island (1851-1916)
Levy, Albert, Little Tancook Island, Nova Scotia (1901-1928)
Levy, Alexander, Little Tancook Island, Nova Scotia (1864-1927)
Levy, George, Little Tancook Island, Nova Scotia (1843-1926)
Levy, Harry, Lunenburg, Nova Scotia (1910-)
Levy, Kingsley, Little Tancook Island, Nova Scotia (1908-)
Levy, Lindsey, Little Tancook Island, Nova Scotia (1892-1980)
Levy, Milford, Little Tancook Island, Nova Scotia (1895-1972)
Levy, W. Raymond, Little Tancook Island, Nova Scotia (1912-1971)
Locke, Charlie, Springbrook, Prince Edward Island (1885-1966)
Loggie, Frank P., Tabusintac, New Brunswick (1862-1939)

MacLennan, William, Tyne Valley, Prince Edward Island (1899-)
MacFarlin, Edwin, Fernwood, Prince Edward Island (1889-1980)
MacInnis, Allen, Port DeRoche, Prince Edward Island (1885-1966)
MacKay, John, Little Harbor, Nova Scotia (circa 1900-1970)
MacKay, Ned, Little Harbor, Nova Scotia (1905-1978)
Marks, Adonijah, New London, Prince Edward Island (1858-1945)
Matt, Gerald, Little Dover, Nova Scotia
May, George, Musquodoboit Harbor, Nova Scotia (circa 1830-1900)
McAvity's Foundry, Saint John, New Brunswick (1834-1960's)
Messenger, Earl, Cape Sable Island, Nova Scotia
Mill, Havelock, Mill's Point, Prince Edward Island (1844-1900)
Mill, W. Roy, Kensington, Prince Edward Island (1901-)
Miller, Eric, St. Elenors, Prince Edward Island (1935-)
Morrison, Archibald, Tabusintac, New Brunswick (1912-1980)
Morrison, George, Tabusintac, New Brunswick (1866-1944)
Moses, Allan, Grand Manan Island, New Brunswick (1881-1953)
Murphy, Alfred, Murphy's Cove, Nova Scotia (1887-1972)

Nickerson, Douglas, Cape Negro, Nova Scotia (1898-)
Nickerson, Fred, Villagedale, Nova Scotia (1902-1980)
Nickerson, Gus, Cape Sable Island, Nova Scotia

Obed, Jesse C., Blanche, Nova Scotia (1878-1932)

Painter, Paul, French River, Prince Edward Island (1925-)
Penny, Rossevelt, Cape Sable Island, Nova Scotia (1933-)
Perry, Enos, Northeast Harbor, Nova Scotia (1879-1975)
Perry, Lloyd, Cape Negro, Nova Scotia (1917-)
Perry, Warren, Cape Negro, Nova Scotia (1912-)
Polchis, William, Kingsclear Indian Reserve, New Brunswick (circa 1855-1935)

Rafuse, Gilbert, Gold River, Nova Scotia (1908-)
Rafuse, Wellington, Fourchu, Nova Scotia (1904-1982)
Ramsay, Frank, Beach Point, Prince Edward Island (1882-1966)
Ramsay, John, Summerside, Prince Edward Island (1858-1934)
Ramsay, Kier, Hamilton, Prince Edward Island (1890-1981)
Ramsay, Ralph, Malpeque, Prince Edward Island (1890-)
Robertson, Willard, Osbourne Harbor, Nova Scotia (1884-1970)
Ross, Allen, Stoney Island, Nova Scotia

Rousseau, Damien, Tabusintac, New Brunswick
Rowlings, William, Musquodoboit Harbor, Nova Scotia (1891-1962)

Sark, Michael "Mick", Lennox Island, Prince Edward Island (1875-1943)
Savoie, Amateur "Mat", Neguac, New Brunswick (1896-)
Sawler, J. Stanley, Western Shore, Nova Scotia (1887-1966)
Selig, Frank, Vogler's Cove, Nova Scotia (1878-1953)
Shupe, Percy, Western Shore, Nova Scotia (1877-1962)
Simmons, Eldred, Lot 16, Prince Edward Island (1918-)
Skerry, George, Lot 16, Prince Edward Island (1916-1965)
Sleunwhite, David, Tancook Island, Nova Scotia
Smith, John, Barrington, Nova Scotia (1882-1968)
Stevens, Daniel, Owl's Head, Nova Scotia (1905-1973)
Stevens, Rudolph, Tancook Island, Nova Scotia (1939-)
Stevens, Vincent, Tancook Island, Nova Scotia (1915-)
Stewart, Ken, Cape Sable Island, Nova Scotia (1891-1969)
Stewart, Noble, Cape Sable Island, Nova Scotia (1929-)
Swim, Romie L., Clark's Harbor, Cape Sable Island, Nova Scotia (1905-1973)
Swimer, Cecil, Gold River, Nova Scotia (1928-)

Tanner, Billy, Stonehurst, Nova Scotia (1913-)
Tanner, Earl, Stonehurst, Nova Scotia (1902-1972)
Tanner, Forbes, Stonehurst, Nova Scotia (1913)
Tanner, Russell Sr., Stonehurst, Nova Scotia (1911-1979)
Tanner, Solomon, Stonehurst, Nova Scotia (1894-)
Thomas, Abram, Lennox Island, Prince Edward Island (1880-1965)
Thompson, Wendall, Long River, Prince Edward Island (1939-)
Tumblin, Irving, Wolf Island, Nova Scotia (1892-1976)

White, Dennis, Stonehurst, Nova Scotia (1899-)
White, Douglas, Bayport, Nova Scotia (1910-)
White, Steven, Lunenburg, Nova Scotia (1912-)
Wilcox, Mariner, Wood Island, New Brunswick (1847-1908)
Wilkins, H.W., Owen Sound, Ontario (1875-1961)
Williams, Burns, Lockeport, Nova Scotia (1906-1981)
Williams, Leonard, Ostrea Lake, Nova Scotia (1883-1967)
Wishart, John L., Tabusintac, New Brunswick (1886-1968)
Wishart, John M., Tabusintac, New Brunswick (1843-1913)

Young, Manson, Tancook Island, Nova Scotia (1883-1933)

Zwicker, Jim, Castalia, Grand Manan Island, New Brunswick (1849-1933)

Plate Index & Credits

Lillianthal Studio is located in Wilton, Maine and Hebb's Photography is located in Bridgewater, Nova Scotia.
Front cover. Decoys: Collection of the authors; photograph by Lillianthal.

PAGE
iv. Map drawn by Walter Meissner.
x. Map drawn by Walter Meissner.
11. Loon: Collection of the authors; photograph by Gary Guyette.
12. Mergansers: Collection of the authors; photograph by Gary Guyette.
13. Warren Tanner and gunning tub: Photograph by Hebb's.
14. Eider: Collection of the authors; photograph by Lillianthal.
15. F. Nickerson portrait: Courtesy of Fred Nickerson.
21. Blair Kaizer portrait: Photograph by Gary Guyette.
23. J. Obed eiders: Collection of the authors; photograph by Lillianthal.
24. J. Obed whistlers: Courtesy of John Matheson; photograph by Gary Guyette.
24. L. Perry eider: Collection of the authors; photograph by Lillianthal.
24. L. Perry scoter: Collection of the authors; photograph by Lillianthal.
25. A. Ross eiders: Collection of Vernon (Ducky) Schnare; photograph by Gary Guyette.
25. L. Perry coot: Private collection; photograph by Lillianthal.
25. E. Hersey eider: Private collection; photograph by Lillianthal.
25. E. Hersey whistler: Collection of Vernon (Ducky) Schnare; photograph by Gary Guyette.
26. W. Perry eider: Collection of the authors; photograph by Lillianthal.
26. Eider: Collection of the authors; photograph by Lillianthal.
26. F. Nickerson whistler: Courtesy of Mrs. Fred Nickerson; photograph by Gary Guyette.
27. Old Squaw: Collection of the authors; photograph by Lillianthal.
27. A. Doan whistlers: Private collection; Photograph by Lillianthal.
27. F. Lamerock merganser: Courtesy of Mrs. Edith Lamerock; photograph by Gary Guyette.
28. F. Lamerock whistlers: Courtesy of Mrs. Edith Lamerock; photograph by Gary Guyette.
28. F. Lamerock eider: Courtesy of Mrs. Edith Lamerock; photograph by Gary Guyette.
28. N. Stuart eiders: Collection of Vernon (Ducky) Schnare; photograph by Gary Guyette.
29. N. Stuart whistler: Collection of Vernon (Ducky) Schnare; photograph by Gary Guyette.
29. K. Stuart whistler: Collection of the authors; photograph by Lillianthal.
29. Eider: Collection of Jamie Stalker; photograph by Gary Guyette.
30. E. Perry whistler: Private collection; photograph by Lillianthal.
30. D. Nickerson eider and blackduck: Private collection; photograph by Lillianthal.
30. O. Crowell eider: Collection of the authors; photograph by Lillianthal.
31. O. Crowell eider: Collection of Mr. and Mrs. Ron Sharp.
31. O. Crowell whistler: Collection of the authors; photograph by Lillianthal.
31. B. Hopkins eider: Collection of the authors; photograph by Lillianthal.
32. J. Smith blackduck: Collection of Mr. and Mrs. Ron Sharp.
32. J. Smith bluebill: Collection of Mr. and Mrs. Ron Sharp.
32. J. Smith whistler: Collection of the authors; photograph by Lillianthal.
32. B. Hopkins eider: Private collection; photograph by Lillianthal.
33. J. Smith eiders: Collection of Mr. and Mrs. Ron Sharp.
33. J. Smith bluebill and whistler: Collection of Vernon (Ducky) Schnare; photograph by Gary Guyette.
33. J. Smith seagull: Collection of Vernon (Ducky) Schnare; photograph by Gary Guyette.
34. R. Penny eiders: Private collection; photograph by Gary Guyette.
34. R. Penny scoter: Collection of the authors; photograph by Lillianthal.
34. R. Penny eider: Collection of the authors; photograph by Lillianthal.
35. E. Messenger merganser: Collection of Vernon (Ducky) Schnare; photograph by Gary Guyette.
35. Loon: Collection of the authors; photograph by Lillianthal.
35. G. Nickerson buffleheads: Collection of Vernon (Ducky) Schnare; photograph by Gary Guyette.
36. R. Swim whistler: Collection of Mr. and Mrs. Ron Sharp.
36. W. Robertson mallards and whistler: Courtesy of Burton and Glen Robertson; photograph by Hebb's.
37. Blackduck: Collection of the authors; photograph by Lillianthal.
37. Harlequin duck: Collection of the authors; photograph by Lillianthal.
37. Whistler: Private collection; photograph by Lillianthal.
38. W. Robertson blackduck and whistler: Collection of the authors; photograph by Lillianthal.
38. W. Robertson whistlers: Collection of the authors; photograph by Lillianthal.
39. B. Williams blackduck: Collection of the authors; photograph by Lillianthal.
39. B. Williams blackduck: Collection of Laurie and Minty Jordan; photograph by Gary Guyette.
39. Whistler: Collection of the authors; photograph by Lillianthal.
40. F. Selig seagull: Collection of Hugh Valiant.
40. Blackduck: Collection of the authors; photograph by Lillianthal.
40. Whistlers: Collection of the authors; photograph by Lillianthal.
41. E. Backman merganser: Collection of Sam and Sally Stewart; photograph by Bernie Gates.
41. Whistler: Private collection; photograph by Lillianthal.
41. R. Levy old squaw: Collection of the authors; photograph by Lillianthal.
42. L. Levy old squaw: Collection of the authors; photograph by Lillianthal.
42. S. and G. Levy old squaws: Private collection; photograph by Lillianthal.

42. S. Levy whistlers: Private collection; photograph by Hebb's.
43. S. Levy bluebills: Private collection; photograph by Hebb's.
43. S. Levy merganser: Private collection; photograph by Hebb's.
43. G. Levy mergansers: Private collection; photograph by Hebb's.
44. R. Levy merganser: Collection of the authors; photograph by Lillianthal.
44. L. Levy blackduck: Private collection; photograph by Hebb's.
44. R. Levy mergansers: Private collection; photograph by Hebb's.
45. R. Levy loon: Collection of the authors; photograph by Lillianthal.
45. R. Levy scoter: Collection of the authors; photograph by Lillianthal.
45. R. Levy whistlers: Collection of the authors; photograph by Lillianthal.
46. R. Levy eiders: Collection of the authors; photograph by Lillianthal.
46. M. Levy scoters: Collection of the authors; photograph by Lillianthal.
47. K. Levy eiders: Courtesy of Phyliss and Kingsley Levy; photograph by Hebb's.
47. K. Levy eider: Collection of the authors; photograph by Lillianthal.
48. A. and K. Levy scoters: Courtesy of Phyliss and Kingsley Levy; photograph by Hebb's.
48. K. Levy scoter: Collection of Norm Marple; photograph by Bernie Gates.
48. K. Levy eiders: Courtesy of Phyliss and Kingsley Levy; photograph by Hebb's.
49. R. Stevens blackduck: Collection of Mr. and Mrs. Harry Porter; photograph by Gary Guyette.
49. R. Stevens seagull: Collection of Jerry Ferguson; photograph by Gary Guyette.
49. M. Young merganser: Collection of Chris Huntington; photograph by Hebb's.
49. M. Young merganser: Collection of the authors; photograph by Lillianthal.
50. R. Stevens blackduck: Collection of Mr. and Mrs. Harry Porter; photograph by Gary Guyette.
50. M. Young loon: Collection of the authors; photograph by Lillianthal.
50. H. Cross merganser: Collection of Laurie and Minty Jordan; photograph by Gary Guyette.
50. Loon: Collection of Mr. and Mrs. R. Casselman.
51. D. Sleunwhite merganser: Private collection; photograph by Lillianthal.
51. V. Stevens mergansers: Collection of Ellen Huntington.
51. Loon: Collection of Mr. and Mrs. Harry Porter; photograph by Gary Guyette.
52. Mergansers: Collection of Laurie and Minty Jordan; photograph by Gary Guyette.
52. Old squaw: Collection of Norman and Andrea Seymour; photograph by Gary Guyette.
52. Bluebill: Collection of Chris Cooper; photograph by Hebb's.
52. Scoters: Private collection; photograph by Lillianthal.
53. Shot box: Collection of Robin Starr; photograph by Robin Starr.
53. S. Tanner eider: Courtesy of Solomon Tanner; photograph by Hebb's.
53. D. White whistlers: Collection of the authors; photograph by Lillianthal.
54. S. White whistlers: Courtesy of Steven White; photograph by Gary Guyette.
54. S. White bluebills: Courtesy of Steven White; photograph by Gary Guyette.
54. D. White blackduck: Collection of Laurie and Minty Jordan; photograph by Gary Guyette.
55. Blackduck: Collection of the authors; photograph by Lillianthal.
55. G. Rafuse merganser: Collection of the authors; photograph by Lillianthal.
55. G. Rafuse old squaw: Collection of Laurie and Minty Jordan; photograph by Gary Guyette.
56. C. Swimer whistler: Private collection; photograph by Lillianthal.
56. C. Swimer merganser: Collection of the authors; photograph by Lillianthal.
56. Tanner merganser: Collection of the authors; photograph by Lillianthal.
56. Eider: Private collection; photograph by Lillianthal.
57. Eiders: Collection of the authors; photograph by Lillianthal.
58. R. Tanner Sr. eiders: Collection of the authors; photograph by Lillianthal.
58. R. Tanner Sr. whistlers: Courtesy of Russell Tanner Jr.; photograph by Hebb's.
58. Stonehurst Harbor: Photograph by Hebb's.
59. Eider: Private collection; photograph by Lillianthal.
59. R. Tanner Sr. blackduck: Courtesy of Russell Tanner Jr.; photograph by Hebb's.
59. Whistlers: Collection of the authors; photograph by Lillianthal.
60. Whistler: Courtesy of Herbert Schiffer antiques.
60. G. Bezanson blackduck: Courtesy of Douglas Bezanson; photograph by Hebb's.
60. G. Bezanson whistlers: Courtesy of Frances and Angus Byers; Hebb's.
61. Old squaw: Courtesy of Mr. and Mrs. R. Casselman.
61. J. Stanley Sawler merganser: Collection of Chris Cooper; photograph by Hebb's.
61. J. Stanley Sawler mergansers: Courtesy of Stan Sawler; photograph by Hebb's.
62. Blair Kaizer blackduck: Collection of the authors; photograph by Lillianthal.
62. J. Stanley Sawler whistlers: Collection of the authors; photograph by Lillianthal.
63. B. Kaizer merganser: Private collection; photograph by Hebb's.
63. Old squaw: Private collection; Photogdraph by Lillianthal.
64. B. Kaizer seagull: Private collection; photo by Hebb's.
64. B. Kaizer merganser: Private collection; photograph by Hebb's.
64. B. Kaizer whistlers: Private collection; photograph by Hebb's.
65. O. Crowell scoter: Collection of Mr. and Mrs. Ron Sharp.
65. O. Crowell scoter: Collection of Mr. and Mrs. Ron Sharp.
66. O. Crowell scoter: Collection of Mr. and Mrs. Ron Sharp.
66. F. Selig blackducks: Collection of Ken Capelle; photograph by Ken Capelle.
67. O. Hiltz merganser: Collection of the authors; photograph by Lillianthal.
67. Brant: Collection of the authors: photograph by Lillianthal.
68. Amateur Savoie blackduck: Collection of C. Blake Lynch; photograph by Lillianthal.
68. H. Mill plover: Collection of the authors; photograph by Lillianthal.
69. E. Backman merganser: Collection of the authors; photograph by Lillianthal.
69. E. Backman whistlers: Collection of John and Shirley Delph, and collection of the authors; photograph by Lillianthal.
70. L. Levy loon: Private collection; photograph by Hebb's.
70. L. Levy mergansers: Private collection; photograph by Hebb's.
71. S. Levy scoter: Private collection; photograph by Hebb's.
71. L. Levy old squaws: Private collection; photograph by Hebb's.
72. Blackduck: Collection of the authors; photograph by Lillianthal.
72. Merganser: Collection of the authors; photograph by Lillianthal.
73. J. Zwicker eiders: Private collection; photograph by Lillianthal.
73. J. Ramsay plover: Collection of the authors; photograph by Lillianthal.
74. F. Nickerson merganser: Collection of the authors; photograph by Lillianthal.
74. Loon: Collection of the authors; photograph by Lillianthal.
75. W. Robertson bluebill and whistler: Collection of the authors; photograph by Lillianthal.
75. W. Robertson mallards: Courtesy of Glen Robertson; photograph by Hebb's.
76. Bluebills: Collection of the authors; photograph by Hebb's.

76. J. Obed eiders: Collection of the authors; photograph by Lillianthal.
77. Old squaw: Collection of Ken Capelle; photograph by Ken Capelle.
77. H. Levy blackduck: Collection of the authors; photograph by Lillianthal.
78. Abram Thomas curlew and yellowlegs: Collection of Arthur and Hazel Clark; photograph by Gary Guyette.
78. J. Ramsay goose: Collection of Alan G. Haid; photograph by Alan G. Haid.
79. Seagull: Collection of Linda and Gene Kangas. Mason dove: Collection of John Weaver.
79. B. Kaizer blackducks: Private collection; photograph by Hebb's.
80. I. Tumblin mergansers: Collection of the authors; photograph by Lillianthal.
80. J. Brooks goose: Collection of the authors; photograph by Lillianthal.
81. P. Shupe mergansers: Collection of the authors; photograph by Lillianthal.
81. P. Shupe whistler: Collection of the authors; photograph by Lillianthal.
82. O. Hiltz whistler: Collection of Jamie Stalker; photograph by Gary Guyette.
82. O. Hiltz mergansers: Collection of the authors; photograph by Lillianthal.
83. O. Hiltz mergansers: Courtesy of James Eisnor; photograph by Hebb's.
83. C. Ernst whistlers: Courtesy of Clarence Ernst; photograph by Hebb's.
83. C. Ernst merganser: Collection of Mr. and Mrs. Harry Porter; photograph by Gary Guyette.
84. C. Ernst mergansers: Collection of Murry Stewart; photograph by Hebb's.
84. O. Hatt merganser: Collection of the authors; photograph by Lillianthal.
84. Merganser: Collection of Chris Cooper; photograph by Hebb's.
85. Geese: Collection of Ralph and Patricia Price.
85. Powder can: Collection of John and Kathy Turnbull; photograph by Gary Guyette.
85. Merganser: Private collection; Hebb's photography.
86. Merganser: Collection of the authors; photograph by Lillianthal.
86. N. and J. MacKay eiders: Private collection; photograph by Lillianthal.
86. Loon: Collection of Jamie Stalker; photograph by Lillianthal.
87. N. MacKay mergansers: Collection of the authors; photograph by Lillianthal.
87. J. MacKay whistlers: Collection of the authors; photograph by Lillianthal.
87. Merganser: Collection of the authors; photograph by Lillianthal.
88. C. Gardiner mergansers: Collection of the authors; photo by Lillianthal.
88. C. Gardiner scoter: Private collection; photograph by Lillianthal.
88. C. Edwards gull: Private collection; photography by Hebb's.
89. C. Edwards blackduck: Private collection; photograph by Hebb's.
89. C. Edwards whistlers: Private collection; photograph by Hebb's.
90. C. Edwards old squaws: Private collection; photograph by Hebb's.
90. C. Edwards scoter: Private collection; photograph by Hebb's.
90. C. Edwards bluebills: Private collection; photograph by Hebb's.
90. A. Murphy scoter and eider: Courtesy of Liegh Murphy; photograph by Hebb's.
91. M. Kaiser blackducks: Private collection; photograph by Richard Field.
91. M. Kaiser whistler: Courtesy of Chris Field; photograph by Hebb's.
91. Hunting photograph: Courtesy of Marshall Kaiser.
92. W. Rowlings yellowlegs: Collection of Jerry Ferguson and collection of the authors; photograph by Gary Guyette.
93. W. Rowlings plover: Collection of John and Shirley Delph; photograph by Shirley Delph.
93. W. Rowlings eider: Private collection; photograph by Gary Guyette.
93. W. Rowlings merganser: Collection of Jim and Mary Richards.
94. R. Baker mergansers: Courtesy of Mr. and Mrs. Jim Baker and Steven Baker; photograph by Gary Guyette.
94. R. Baker scoter: Courtesy of Chris Field; photograph by Hebb's.
94. G. May harlequin duck: Collection of Laurie and Minty Jordan; photograph by Gary Guyette.
94. Goose: Private collection; photograph by Lillianthal.
95. L. Williams goose: Collection of the authors; photograph by Lillianthal.
95. Gull: Collection of the authors; photograph by Lillianthal.
95. Eider: Collection of the authors; photograph by Lillianthal.
95. D. Stevens whistlers: Private collection; photograph by Lillianthal.
96. L. Burt eiders: Collection of the authors; photograph by Lillianthal.
96. Whistler and scoter: Collection of the authors; photograph by Lillianthal.
96. Eider and whistlers: Collection of the authors; photograph by Lillianthal.
97. Mergansers: Collection of Laurie and Minty Jordon; photograph by Gary Guyette.
97. Scoter: Private collection; photograph by Lillianthal.
97. Loon: Collection of Jamie Stalker; photograph by Gary Guyette.
98. H. Burke eider: Collection of the authors; photograph by Lillianthal.
98. Eider and scoter: Collection of John and Hilary McKay; photograph by Gary Guyette.
99. Eider: Collection of Laurie and Minty Jordan; photograph by Gary Guyette.
99. G. Matt merganser: Collection of Laurie and Minty Jordan; photograph by Gary Guyette.
99. Teal: Private collection; photograph by Lillianthal.
100. W. Rafuse eiders: Private collection; photograph by Gary Guyette.
100. W. Rafuse merganser: Collection of the authors; photograph by Lillianthal.
100. E. Langille blackduck: Collection of the authors; photograph by Lillianthal.
101. Merganser: Private collection; photograph by Hebb's.
101. Plover: Collection of the authors; photograph by Lillianthal.
102. Mergansers: Private collection; photograph by Gary Guyette.
102. Map drawn by Walter Meissner.
103. J. Brooks plover: Private collection; photograph by Gary Guyette.
104. North Shore Hotel; photograph by Gary Guyette.
105. J. Ramsay brant: Private collection and collection of the authors; photograph by Lillianthal.
106. Spring hunting: Painted by Virginia Guyette.
108. A. Holland photograph: Courtesy of Mrs. Ruth Shapiro.
109. A. Holland photograph: Courtesy of Mrs. Ruth Shapiro.
111. J. Brooks photograph: Courtesy of John Ramsay.
113. R. Ramsay portrait: Photograph by Gary Guyette.
115. J. Ramsay brant (left): Private collection; photograph by Lillianthal.
115. J. Ramsay brant (right): Collection of the authors; photograph by Lillianthal.
116. & 117. J. Ramsay geese: Collection of the authors; photograph by Lillianthal.
117. J. Ramsay plover: Collection of the authors; photograph by Lillianthal.
118. J. Ramsay goose: Private collection.
118. Plover: Collection of the authors; photograph by Lillianthal.
119. J. Brooks goose: Collection of the authors; photograph by Lillianthal.
119. J. Brooks brant: Collection of Jamie Stalker; photograph by Gary Guyette.
120. J. Brooks brant: Private collection; photograph by Gary Guyette.
120. J. Brooks brant: Private collection; photograph by Gary Guyette.

165. A. Savoie brant: Collection of John and Hilary McKay; Photograph by Gary Guyette.
165. A. Savoie goose: Collection of Al Minucci; photograph by Al Minucci.
166. A. Savoie blackduck: Collection of John and Hilary McKay; photograph by Gary Guyette.
166. A. Savoie blackducks: Collection of John and Hilary McKay; photograph by Gary Guyette.
166. A. Savoie goose: Collection of John and Hilary McKay; photograph by Gary Guyette.
167. A. Savoie blackduck: Collection of John and Hilary McKay; photograph by Gary Guyette.
167. A. Savoie whistlers: Collection of John and Hilary McKay; photograph by Gary Guyette.
167. A. Savoie whistler: Collection of John and Kathy Turnbull; photograph by Gary Guyette.
168. J. Gagnon goose: Collection of John and Hilary McKay; photograph by Gary Guyette.
168. J.L. Wishart cormorant: Collection of John and Hilary McKay; photograph by Gary Guyette.
168. P. Ginnish brant: Collection of John and Hilary McKay; photograph by Gary Guyette.
169. P. Ginnish goose: Collection of John and Kathy Turnbull; photograph by Gary Guyette.
169. J. Gatreau goose: Collection of the authors; photograph by Lillianthal.
170. J. Gatreau blackduck and goose: Collection of the authors; photograph by Lillianthal.
170. T. McAvity brant: Collection of John and Kathy Turnbull; photograph by Gary Guyette.
170. F. Loggie brant: Collection of John and Hilary McKay; photograph by Gary Guyette.
171. T. McAvity brant: Courtesy of Lorne Wishart; photograph by Gary Guyette.
171. J. Bailey goose: Courtesy of Lorne Wishart; photograph by Gary Guyette.
171. J. Bailey brant: Collection of the authors; photograph by Lillianthal.
172. Goose: Collection of the authors; photograph by Gary Guyette.
172. W. Polchis blackduck: Collection of John and Hilary McKay; photograph by Gary Guyette.
172. A. Landry brant: Collection of John and Hilary McKay; photograph by Gary Guyette.
173. A. Morrison goose: Private collection; photograph by Lillianthal.
173. A. Morrison brant and blackduck: Collection of John and Hilary McKay; photograph by Gary Guyette.
173. Goose: Collection of John and Hilary McKay; photograph by Gary Guyette.
174. A. Doucette goose: Private collection; photograph by Gary Guyette.
174. C. Johnson blackduck: Collection of John and Hilary McKay; photograph by Gary Guyette.
174. C. Johnson geese: Collection of the authors; photograph by Lillianthal.
175. Goose: Collection of the authors; photograph by Lillianthal.
175. E.L. Goodwin goose: Collection of the authors; photograph by Lillianthal.
175. E.L. Goodwin goose: Collection of John and Hilary McKay; photograph by Gary Guyette.
176. R. Howlett goose: Collection of John and Hilary McKay; photograph by Gary Guyette.
176. R. Howlett whistlers: Collection of John and Hilary McKay; photograph by Gary Guyette.
176. F. Duvernet blackduck: Collection of John and Hilary McKay; photograph by Gary Guyette.
177. Whistlers: Collection of John and Hilary Mc Kay; photograph by Gary Guyette.
177. Blackduck: Collection of John and Kathy Turnbull; photograph by Gary Guyette.
177. Blackduck: Collection of John and Kathy Turnbull; photograph by Gary Guyette.
178. J. Beckett goose: Collection of John and Hilary McKay; photograph by Gary Guyette.
178. H. Gilbert blackduck and whistler: Private collection; photograph by Gary Guyette.
178. Whistler: Collection of John and Hilary McKay; photograph by Gary Guyette.
179. H.W. Wilkins bluebills: Collection of John and Hilary McKay; photograph by Gary Guyette.
179. H.W. Wilkins blackduck: Collection of C. Blake Lynch; photograph by Gary Guyette.
180. D. Rousseau goose: Collection of John and Kathy Turnbull; photograph by Gary Guyette.
180. Goose: Private collection; photograph by Gary Guyette.
180. Blackduck: Collection of John and Kathy Turnbull; photograph by Gary Guyette.
181. Unfinished decoy: Collection of the authors; photograph by Lillianthal.
181. Blackduck: Private collection; photograph by Gary Guyette.
181. Blackduck: Collection of John and Kathy Turnbull; photograph by Gary Guyette.
182. Goose: Collection of the authors; photograph by Lillianthal.
182. Whistlers: Courtesy of Marcia Ross; photograph by Hebb's.
182. A. Moses old squaw: Courtesy of G.W. Anderson; photograph by Gary Guyette.
183. M. Wilcox old squaws: Private collection; photograph by Gary Guyette.
183. Auk: Collection of Jim and Mary Richards.
183. J. Green mergansers and whistlers: Private collection; photograph by Gary Guyette.
184. L. Harvey blackduck: Courtesy of Lincoln Harvey; photograph by Gary Guyette.
184. L. Harvey blackduck and whistler: Courtesy of Lincoln Harvey; photograph by Gary Guyette.
184. Eiders: Private collection; photograph by Lillianthal.
184. Gunners box: Collection of John and Kathy Turnbull; photograph by Gary Guyette.
185. Art Holland: Courtesy of Mrs. Ruth Shapiro.

Back cover. Decoys: Collection of the authors; photograph by Lillianthal.
Back cover. Coastal scene: Photograph by Hebb's.

Index